Group Transformation

GROUP TRANSFORMATION

An Analysis
of a Learning Group

THEODORE M. MILLS
Yale University

PRENTICE-HALL, INC. *Englewood Cliffs, New Jersey*

301.15 LC
6519
M56

PRENTICE-HALL INTERNATIONAL, INC., *London*
PRENTICE-HALL OF AUSTRALIA, PTY., LTD., *Sydney*
PRENTICE-HALL OF CANADA, LTD., *Toronto*
PRENTICE-HALL OF INDIA (PRIVATE) LTD., *New Delhi*
PRENTICE-HALL OF JAPAN, INC., *Tokyo*
PRENTICE-HALL DE MEXICO, S.A., *Mexico City*

Library of Congress
Catalog Card No.: 64-21464

PRINTED IN THE UNITED STATES OF AMERICA
36547-C

Preface

This book describes the transformations of a single group as it gathers, forms, operates, and dissolves and as these changes are detected by a systematic analysis of the content of each event that occurs. Empirical trends lead to a conception of the life cycle of groups which I hope will serve as a useful guide to leaders, members, and those interested in human groups. One aim of the discussion is to suggest both the feasibility and the practical value of systematic collection of group process data.

Another is to point up certain realities of group change which deserve more attention from the social system theorist. For example, most small groups are transitory. They originate, and they terminate. Their boundaries form, and they dissolve. Although members must face the practical and emotional realities of dissolution, modern theory has not taken it into full account. In fact, most theories are predicated upon the assumption that boundaries will be maintained, that dissolution does not occur. Are transitory groups so special that they require a separate theory, or should our general theories be modified to accommodate the transformations observed in such groups?

By an empirical analysis of processes in a single group, the book raises this and other questions relevant to general social science theory.

For patience and skill in learning and applying the content scheme, I am deeply grateful to Miss Nancy E. Waxler of the Massachusetts Mental Health Center.

Basic data from classificatory schemes cannot, of course, speak for themselves, but must be interpreted. One needs either a comprehensive and incisive theory, or, in its absence (the unfortunate and current case in small groups), notions and ideas that have at least stood the tests of tough and imaginative discussion. For ideas of this caliber I am indebted to two groups of associates. The first group consists of fellow instructors in the group discussion course at Harvard University, known formerly as Social Science 112, Human Relations, and currently as Social Relations 120, Case Analysis— The Interpretation of Interpersonal Behavior: Hugh Cabot, Philip E. Slater, Charles P. Whitlock, and, at a later period, Kiyo Morimoto, Robert F. Bales, and Richard D. Mann. Their search for an effective teaching milieu and for an understanding of how students' group experience affects their thought has been invaluable to me. I want to thank the latter five for their encouragement when the preliminary content trends were reviewed in Cambridge in the spring of 1961. Research associates of Dr. Elvin V. Semrad of the Massachusetts Mental Health Center are the second group: John Arsenian, Warren G. Bennis, David Shapiro, and William Schutz. In studying the processes in Dr. Semrad's training groups for psychiatrists in residence in the Boston area, their discussions of central group issues and of likely developmental trends were of special importance. I am grateful to both these groups and to Dr. Semrad for introducing me to a psychoanalytical view of the group. I want to thank Philip E. Slater, Richard D. Mann, and Warren G. Bennis, again, and Walter W. Igersheimer for helpful critiques of the draft of the manuscript.

Financial support for the investigation was given by the U.S. Department of Health, Education and Welfare, through National Institutes of Health research grant M-3876.

Contents

Contents

Introduction

Interest in small groups has produced at least four specialized modes of inquiry: (1) controlled experimentation in the laboratory;[1] (2) analysis in the "field" or in organizational settings;[2] (3) clinical analysis, stimulated by but not restricted to psycho-

[1] For a classification of and reference to a series of studies, see M. E. Roseborough, "Experimental Studies of Small Groups," *Psychological Bulletin,* L (1953), 275-303. For superior anthologies, including important comments on the field, see Dorwin Cartwright and Alvin Zander, eds., *Group Dynamics,* 2nd ed. (New York: Harper & Row, Publishers, 1960); A. Paul Hare, Edgar F. Borgatta, and Robert F. Bales, eds., *Small Groups* (New York: Alfred A. Knopf, Inc., 1955); J. H. Rohr and M. Sherif, eds., *Social Psychology at the Crossroads* (New York: Harper & Row, Publishers, 1951); H. Guetzkow, ed., *Groups, Leadership and Man* (Pittsburgh: Carnegie Press, 1951); and A. Paul Hare, *Handbook of Small Group Research* (New York: The Free Press of Glencoe, Inc., 1962).

[2] For example, see the pioneering study by F. J. Roethlisberger and W. J. Dickson, *Management and the Worker* (Cambridge, Mass.: Harvard University Press, 1939); also W. F. Whyte, *Street Corner Society* (Chicago: University of Chicago Press, 1943); George Homans, "The Cash Posters: A Study of a Group of Working Girls," *American Sociological Review,* XIX (1954), 724-33; Lester Coch and John R. P. French, Jr., "Overcoming Resistance to Change," *Human Relations,* I (1948), 512-32; Seymour M. Lipset, Martin A. Trow, and James S. Coleman, *Union Democracy* (New York: The Free Press of Glencoe, Inc., 1956); and Edward A. Shils, "Primary Groups in the American Army," in *Studies in the Scope and Method of "The American Soldier,"* eds. Robert K. Merton and Paul F. Lazarsfeld (New York: The Free Press of Glencoe,

analytical interpretation of therapy and training groups;[3] and (4) application of systematic classificatory schemes for comparing frequencies and trends of events through time and across groups.[4] Although specialists may share certain interests, they do not easily commute from one mode to another. Gaps exist because interests, assumptions, techniques, theoretical framework, and contacts with groups differ; for example, the gap between laboratory and field has been a major concern.[5] Just as perplexing is the one separating clinical interpretation from systematic classification, separating the clinician who unravels the manifold significances of group events from the observer who sorts, counts, and adds up acts.

The clinician's aim is to comprehend what is going on in the group. His mode is to dissect, disentangle, and decipher on manifest and latent, conscious and unconscious, cognitive and symbolic levels the whences, the whys, the functions, and the consequences of as small a bit of life as the single event. His explorations are often wide ranging, free associating, and yet painstaking. For instance, he may observe that Harold, a member of a training group, makes a slip of the tongue. For several sessions the group has been split over the admission into the group of an institutional official. In referring to him, Harold, by mistake, uses the training instructor's name. As the group laughs, he corrects himself and sinks down in his chair. How is one to understand this event? What does it express about Harold's feelings toward the official, toward the instructor, toward the group? What conception of internal and external boundaries of the group does it convey? Why does it occur at this moment? Is it related to the instructor's previous absence? to the

---

Inc., 1950). For an introduction to field experiments, see John R. P. French, Jr., "Experiments in Field Settings," in *Research Methods in the Behavioral Sciences*, eds. Leon Festinger and Daniel Katz (New York: Dryden Press, 1953), Chap. 3, pp. 98-135.

[3] W. R. Bion, *Experiences in Groups* (New York: Basic Books, Inc., 1961), pp. 41-75; S. H. Foulkes and E. J. Anthony, *Group Psychotherapy* (London: Penguin Books, Ltd., 1957).

[4] E. D. Chapple, "The Measurement of Interpersonal Behavior," *Transactions of the New York Academy of Science*, IV (1942), 222-33; Robert F. Bales, *Interaction Process Analysis* (Reading, Mass.: Addison-Wesley Publishing Co., Inc., 1950); B. Steinzor, "The Development and Evaluation of a Measure of Social Interaction," *Human Relations*, Part 1, II (1949), 103-21; and Part 2 in II (1949), 319-47.

[5] Leon Festinger, "Laboratory Experiments," in *Research Methods*, eds. Festinger and Katz, pp. 137-72; Sidney Verba, *Small Groups and Political Behavior* (Princeton, N.J.: Princeton University Press, 1961).

current absence of a member? What is its resonance in the group, as suggested by the laughter? These and many more questions might be raised by the clinical observer. He may be led to one or more hypotheses, for example, that the slip, among other things, expresses the feeling that the real issue was the division in the group over whether they should admit into their group the training instructor sitting before them, not the hospital official. Rarely can the clinician prove that his interpretation is right or wrong or that it is the best of a number of explanations; but, in this instance, the fact that the group never again raised the question of admitting the official is, indeed, relevant evidence.

The clinician soon learns that a group event, contrary to a common assumption, gives not too few leads but too many, which come at too fast a rate to be adequately understood. He learns that comprehending the here and now, as recorded by tape or film, is exceedingly hard work—work that taxes one's intellect, imagination, emotions, theory, and professional schedule. Not many people can spend many hours doing it. Its difficulty is increased by another factor, namely, that the clinician's personal feelings about group members, the instructor, and so on, find their way into his interpretations so that he must understand his own relations with the group as well. Seeking objective confirmation of his ideas in the judgment of peers, he may present them to a group specially formed to study groups only to find that *that* group must be analyzed in order to make sense of its reaction to him and so on, perhaps, ad infinitum. Because the mechanical attempt to speed up digestive action by pooling clinical experience simply multiplies the rate at which undigested events occurs, the problem seems to be boundless.

Comprehension of the particular is demanded by one's professional role in the sense that most often clinical observers have been, are, or expect to be, leaders, teachers, or therapists. Consequently, they are, or anticipate being, active members of groups, and as such, will want and are expected to intervene. Their actions will be instructive, therapeutic, or otherwise, depending upon their comprehension of what is going on. With so much of group process still unknown and unformulated, the probability of missing the point necessitates caution in drawing conclusions, openness in entertaining hypotheses, facility in shifting from level to level, and sensitivity to emotional processes which are still not satisfactorily understood. Quite appropriately, a central theme in training a group practitioner and a clinical observer is the prevention of premature closure. His training and responsibility being what it is, it is not surprising that as he encounters the systematic observer he becomes impatient with the "superficial" classificatory schemes which by their nature must be "closed" before observation begins.

The systematic observer approaches the group with a set of categories and a manual. Often his categories are like a row of hoppers, into one of which he tosses each discernible group event. His task is to sort accurately and well, according to the manual. The simplicity and arbitrariness of his operation usually belies the history of a scheme's development. Pretesting may have begun with an entirely different set of categories; integration with a theoretical scheme may have required modification; reliability tests may have indicated the need to drop some distinctions and introduce others; and human limitations of scorers may have forced additional simplifications or changes. A scheme's history may contain a series of compromises, each attempting to accommodate demands from theory, reliability, practicality, and so forth. Ordinarily, however, the scheme's applicability to a variety of groups operating in widely different circumstances is not compromised, for if the clinician is oriented chiefly to the complexities of the here and now, the systematic observer has an eye to the extensive population of groups for which he feels his scheme is relevant. His interest in the present group is comparative, for it is mainly through comparisons that he is able to determine the generality of his readings. Such comparison is not possible, of course, unless the scoring scheme is to a certain extent, and even to a great extent, free from the complexities of the here and now. Unencumbered by the manifold properties of an event, but guided by a general set of concepts, the scheme enables the investigator to say, Whatever X is, there is more of it here than there. If X is what I think it is, then this situation more nearly approaches condition A than does that situation. The principles to which this approach contributes are abstract and general. The systematician's professional role as scientist speeds him past the full significance of a single event, indeed, of a single group, and on to more and more groups. His responsibility entails many thousands of events in many hundreds of groups.

The gap between the systematician and the clinician tends to widen because it is more than accidental or a matter of taste and talent or merely the consequence of a past history of separate schools, different teachers, and different subcultures. It is not a matter that will be alleviated by natural progressive developments because the clinician and the systematician have accepted responsibility in professional roles which demand different orientations to groups; and because along with realistic doubts that the current *results* of the work each have practical utility for the other is the feeling that each has, in some manner, gone beyond the other. How, the clinician asks, can one classify something until one knows what it is and the way in which it is significant? In return, the systematician asks, what knowledge is produced by rearranging one's frame of reference each time a new series of events appears?

In spite of the forces separating them—and not just because of their differences—each has something to learn from the other. For his part, the clinician may understand more fully the sociology of the group before him. At present, his most substantial and dependable theoretical basis (although by no means the only one used) is the set of models of the personality system. Some see no need for any other concepts. De Schill, commenting on Foulkes's suggested application of group concepts, states, "We analysts are quite capable of accurately describing the existing relationship in the basic group, namely, the family, without referring to terms such as 'gestalt,' 'group mind,' and others. Their use regarding the therapeutic group is therefore both unnecessary and misleading." [6] Others are fearful that conceptions of the group and its properties will obliterate the individual as an object of interest and consequently subvert the therapeutic enterprise. Taking what must be understood as an extremely narrow definition of group dynamics, Schwartz contends,

> The group dynamic point of view sponsors a false belief in the value of mediocrity. The group dynamic orientation is antirational and antimultidimensional. It emphasizes structures and neglects content and process. The stress on group dynamics is anticlinical and antitherapeutic in its devaluation of history and diagnosis. . . . Any therapy which does not attend to the individual, *his*

---

[6] In discussing S. H. Foulkes, "The Application of Group Concepts to the Treatment of the Individual in the Group," *Topical Problems of Psychotherapy,* II (Basle, Switzerland: S. Karger, 1960), 50.

[7] Emanuel K. Schwartz and Alexander Wolf, "Psychoanalysis in Groups:

history, *his* psychodynamics, *his* dreams, *his* pathology, and *his* health remains superficial.[7]

In reply, one might ask the nature of that therapy (or any other kind of enterprise in groups) which chooses to perceive, interpret, and account for all events in terms only of their significance to a disjoined aggregate of personality systems, each intricately structured within but unconnected to one another—except in those ways which seem important to what is within. In due regard to the immense difficulty of unraveling the strands of the psychodynamics of the individual, and consequently of the necessity for dealing only with those matters which seem to be of the utmost significance, even the crudest counting system shows that group processes are highly organized.[8] An interaction system of some sort unquestionably exists. The behavior of one person is conditional upon the nature of that system, not just upon actions of a significant other. Quite apart from other aspects of the group, interdependence on this level exemplifies a kind of order which cannot be reduced to terms of the personality system. True (it may be argued), but it is not important how many times a person acts; it is what he says, what he feels, what is going on inside. If theoretical sociologists are correct, interdependence extends far beyond and far below overt interaction. Ideas become structured in an indigenous culture containing central values and a

---

The Mystique of Group Dynamics," *Topical Problems*, p. 131.

[8] In Robert F. Bales *et al.*, "Channels of Communication in Small Groups," *American Sociological Review*, XVI (1951), 461-68, it is shown that when members are ranked by their activity output, their rank in receiving comments from others corresponds, and that within pairs there is regularly an imbalance such that the lower ranking member directs more acts to the higher ranking one than he receives from him in return. F. F. Stephan and E. G. Mishler, in "The Distribution of Participation in Small Groups: An Exponential Approximation," *American Sociological Review*, XVII (1952), 598-608, report that the distribution follows a simple exponential model. That position within the participation matrix is related to emotional and thought processes is suggested by Theodore M. Mills, "Developmental Processes in Three-person Groups," *Human Relations*, IX (1956), 343-55, where it is found that the high participator (within a coalition in the triad) creates more than his share of negative fantasy; the middle, more than his share of positive; and the low, more than his share of neutral. One need not go to these or other references to demonstrate that the individual within an organization acts, thinks, and feels with a sensitivity to that organization. Every team athlete knows it. The point is not this, but rather that seemingly chaotic processes may possess a high degree of organization which escapes us because of the limitations of our conceptual schemes.

hierarchy of norms for evaluating behavior. Norms and behavior become married to persons in the form of roles, and an intricate pattern of role relations becomes established. On a more latent level, loves and animosities press for pairs, triangles, and other formations which constitute an arrangement of their own, a structure which is reinforced by ancient and contemporary taboos.

The ramification of this interdependence into the more latent levels of the group is suggested by Foulkes and Anthony when they say, "The compelling currents of ancient tribal feeling" permeate "to the very core and . . . all subsequent interactions are inescapably embedded in this common matrix. . . . The group is a more fundamental unit than the individual which goes beyond the more usual emphasis on interpersonal relationships and reactions." [9] Bion conceives of shared, unconscious, basic assumptions which are experienced by group members, quite apart from their needs and wishes, and which transform the members into a specialized, recognizable state.[10]

Certainly, each personality participates in this latent affective system (just as it does in role relations, in the group's culture, and in its interaction system), but these various subsystems themselves cannot be explained by personality-system theory, neither by analyzing each person of the aggregate separately, then adding them up (any more than one can account fully for the solar system by a linear analysis of each planet) nor by transplanting the personality model upon the group as a whole, relying upon temporary substitutes for concepts such as group superego, group mentality, and so on.[11] Scheidlinger suggests that the fundamental problem is to relate—not substitute one for the other—group phenomena and the personalities of group members.[12] The relationship of these matters requires a theory of its own, one which we do not yet have.

All well and good, one might say, but will not adding notions of sociological systems only confuse an already complicated interpretive apparatus? Until the theories are clear, incisive, and workable, this is likely to be the case; but even before that time recognition of

---

[9] Quoted by Schwartz and Wolf, "Psychoanalysis in Groups," *Topical Problems*, p. 124.

[10] Bion, *Experiences in Groups*, pp. 41-75.

[11] Schwartz and Wolf, "Psychoanalysis in Groups," *Topical Problems*, p. 151.

[12] S. Scheidlinger, "Group Process in Group Psychotherapy" (New York: Annual meeting, Group Psychotherapy Association, January 1958).

the issue may, on occasion, simply make explicit the bases for interpretation already implicitly used. An example is the slip of the
tongue mentioned previously. If the slip serves as a comment upon
the previous discussion, it is as much a cultural event as it is an
unconscious expression, cultural in the sense that it gives an entirely new meaning to much that has been said before and consequently alters the accumulated culture. As such it has both psychological and sociological significance. With an additional frame of
reference, the practicing clinician may strengthen his teaching or
therapeutic role by interpreting events, not only for personalities,
but also for their significance to the interaction system, to group
culture, to the normative system, and to the latent affective system.
This is essentially what is done implicitly when one seeks to understand transference relations.

For his part, in exchange, the systematician may become more
fully aware of what he is and is not counting, of what facets of
group process are and are not countable. Despite education to the
contrary, it is rare that the abstract categorizer escapes entirely the
assumption that significant properties of the system consist of only
those which he abstracts. One begins to believe that group phenomena occur irrespective of people and that the group is no more
than what can be seen, heard, and scored. This belief is encouraged
by the fact that it is easier to classify an act than it is to assess the
silent currents associated with it—the unvoiced definitions, evaluations, and feelings. Classification of the overt is easier to judge than
the service it performs and the demands it makes. To score easier
things first is probably wise, but closure for technical reasons often
inadvertently becomes theoretical closure. The systematician can
learn from the clinician those areas and levels that the former is
failing to tap. This knowledge is of immense practical value, for if
those untapped areas are major sources of variance, they are precisely the ones which he must either control or take into account in
order to make meaningful comparisons across sets of groups.

If one were to anticipate for a moment the future course of social
science and imagine a group theory—or a set of theories—at once
incisive for the immediate moment, inclusive of the various levels
upon which group currents operate, incorporating a variety of types
of groups, and general enough to generate further fruitful deduc-

tions, then a fifth gap becomes apparent: the one separating this general theory from the fragmentary, conceptual schemes of clinician and systematician alike. In fact, one can add to these schemes those of the experimentalist and the field investigator, for, when compared to a general theory, a major feature all four areas have in common is particularistic, fragmentary theories.

As suggested above, exchange between specialists can do something to bridge the gap between them,[13] but just as barter by itself brings no new products, exchange alone may not be enough. For one thing, the professional roles would remain essentially the same. A more creative bridging is called for, namely, for specialists— whether jointly or separately, it does not matter—to assume the *additional* role of thinking their formulations through to the point where they contribute to a theory that has general use.[14]

A step in this direction is taken in this study, which reports the results of a systematic analysis of the content in a group-discussion course at Harvard University, interprets content trends in terms thought to be familiar to clinical observers, and draws several implications for a general theory of groups.

Chapter 1 briefly introduces the group. Chapter 2 introduces the method of content analysis, including its scoring operations, its classification of objects; its categories of the positive, the negative,

[13] Therapists and systematic observers have worked together to apply systematic observation technique to therapy groups; outstanding examples are J. T. Evans, "Objective Measurement of the Therapeutic Group Process" (Ph.D. dissertation, Harvard University, 1950); G. A. Talland, "Task and Interaction Process: Some Characteristics of Therapeutic Group Discussion," *Journal of Abnormal and Social Psychology*, L (1955), 105-9; George Psathas, "Interaction Process Analysis of Two Psychotherapy Groups, "*International Journal of Group Psychotherapy*, X (1960), 430-55; George Psathas, "Phase Movement and Equilibrium Tendencies in Interaction Process Analysis in Psychotherapy Groups," *Sociometry*, XXIII (June 1960), 177-94. None of these studies would claim to have fused the clinical and systematic viewpoints; in fact, the difficulty in comprehending the significance of the findings for the lives of group members, for the therapeutic process, and for the therapist attests, again, to the gap.

[14] Foulkes and Anthony, and in particular Bion, have made important contributions in this regard. The fact that their formulations have met with so much misunderstanding, confusion, and acrimony, as exemplified by papers in *Topical Problems in Psychotherapy*, may be explained as one might prefer in psychodynamic or group-dynamic terms; but in any case it attests to a void— to the absence of a general and effective way of thinking about group phenomena.

and the neutral; its reliability; and its theoretical grounding in semantics and sociology. Over-all totals for the Harvard group are reported.

In Chapter 3, we follow the session-by-session readings in positive and negative scores and, as a first approximation, suggest the kind of group processes that are manifest in the content expressed by the members. As a second approximation, certain central group issues are formulated in Chapter 4, and general trends are interpreted as reflections of how these issues are confronted and handled by this particular group. These interpretations lead in the next chapter to a general formulation of the life cycle of learning, training, and similar groups. Chapter 6 shifts from changes *of* the group to changes *in* it. It brings content data to bear upon (1) Bales' hypothesis regarding adaptive and integrative changes[15] and (2) the dynamic connection between the group's interpersonal processes and its view of the external world. The final chapter summarizes the main points of the study and draws three theoretical conclusions.

[15] Robert F. Bales, "Adaptive and Integrative Changes as Sources of Strain in Social Systems," in *Small Groups*, pp. 127-31.

1

The Group

Students from Harvard and Radcliffe Colleges compose the group, which is one of four sections of a full-year course entitled "Social Relations 120, Case Analysis: The Interpretation of Interpersonal Behavior" and formally known as Social Science 112. The schedule calls for 68 one-hour sessions, at 9:00 in the morning on Mondays, Wednesdays, and Fridays from September 28, 1959, to May 4, 1960.

The classroom is well windowed and well lighted and has an accoustical tile ceiling with a microphone suspended at its center. The line leads to a tape recorder beside the door. Students enter, some taking seats around a U-shaped set of tables, others in chairs forming an outer U by the wall. The instructor sits on the desk which is placed at the opening of the inner U.

"My name is Mills and this course is Social Relations 120. Its aim is to develop our skills in observing and understanding more fully concrete instances of human behavior. My role is to assist in this process.

"The materials we will deal with are of three sorts: first, the cases which are instances occurring in real life and written up by persons who were directly involved. Some of them, a good proportion of them, are written by former students in this course, for one of our assignments in the spring is to write up a case from our own experience and to present an analysis of it.

"I suggest for Wednesday and Friday of this week we discuss the first case, called *The Michaelson Family*. I suggest that we raise the questions of what is happening and why persons are behaving as they are.

"The second set of materials is the readings. You will see that the first part contains selections from Fromm, from Piaget, from Freud, and from Schachtel. I suggest that we leave Monday, October 19, open so that we can raise questions in the group here about special problems you have encountered in the readings. From the list you will see that later on we will have selections from Leary, Hayakawa, Bateson, Baruch, Malinowski, and other selections from Freud.

"The third set of materials consists of events which take place here in our group. What we do here can be seen in itself as a case. Part of our task will be to understand what we find ourselves doing as a group, to understand why we do it as we do. I suggest that after we discuss the Michaelsons and the second case, called *The Seitons*, we leave a session free to go back over what has happened in our own group.

"There will be an hour exam on November 9 and an examination covering cases, readings, and our own processes as a group at midyear. There is a spring paper—the personal case I mentioned earlier—and a final examination covering the entire year.

"You will notice the microphone and the tape recorder. It is customary in this course to record all sessions, and at this time I would like to introduce in the back of the room, Mr. Porter, a graduate student who is interested in group processes and who asked to be here during the course. His role is as an observer, and I suggest that our relationship to him be as though he were furniture.

"These are the things I have to say now. Do you have any questions?"

A long and, as someone later reports, painful silence follows. Finally a woman student asks, "In reading a case what should we look for?" Other questions follow: "What kinds of problems are involved in the cases?" "Will we analyze something like *Long Day's Journey Into Night*?" "Do we get into a psychoanalysis of the individual?" "What do you mean by an analysis of a case?" "Is there any short, compact volume containing all the necessary psychological terms?" "Are we trying to find out general rules, general principles?" "What are we supposed to get out of the course?"

A girl remarks, "I gather we are not supposed to rely upon others, like Freud and all. This is our own—our own ideas and all."

At the end of the hour a male student sitting opposite the instructor at the center of the U touches off general laughter when he asks, "Am I to assume that you are not willing to direct the discussion?"

Hypotheses about what is going on, what the group is, what it should be, what role the instructor is taking, what the group is likely to become—such tentative queries and formulations are first steps in the kind of learning introduced by the course; for as Perry has suggested, the course

> . . . attempts to illuminate principles and complexities at the very point at which the student has the greatest vested interest —the understanding of causation in the immediate daily behavior of people. This is a subject on which the student, to be a reasonably confident social animal, *must* already have a set of beliefs sufficient to account for almost all the normal expectancies of his life . . . and he must trust them. Tell him about the spiral nebulae, and he is eager. With only minor rebellion he will "discover" modern art or the Old Masters. He can learn to be flexible and tolerant of change on the periphery, for he can control the rate at which these changes permeate his being. But question his conviction about who is the villain in a fraternity scandal [or about how the teacher should lead a discussion course or about who has the right to speak on what subject—I would add] . . . and you have asked him to consider whether the next step will really be there as he descends the stairs in his own home.[1]

> The central purpose of the course is not to change students' ways of life. . . . Its purpose is to develop in them a primarily intellectual function, which, like most others, can be evidenced in written documents. It just happens, unfortunately, that many students have to change their feelings about life . . . in order to develop this function.[2]

> The single, objective case, as the object of joint study, provides . . . levers of great power for the uprooting of preconceptions

---

[1] William G. Perry, Jr., "The 'Human Relations' Course in the Curriculum of Liberal Arts," *The Journal of General Education*, IX, No. 1 (October 1935), 7.

[2] Perry, "The 'Human Relations' Course," *Journal of General Education*, p. 8.

and prejudices, while at the same time it provides controls over the evils of this power. The case itself is the fulcrum of leverage. When disagreement arises in the group, it is quite impossible to escape its implications by the usual rationalizations referring to other irrelevant data or by "permitting" differences in something vaguely and comfortingly called "opinion." It is even impossible to retreat for long into the smoke of self-righteous passion. All these conventional outcomes of argument are designed to leave the participants with at least one human bond left, the notion that we all see the same "thing" (or would if we had the same data), even if we often have different opinions "about" it or even if the other fellow is a bit pigheaded at times. The "case," however, provides a circumscribed set of data, and, through the instructor's patient insistence that it be looked at and looked at again, the discussion reveals to the students that, as they looked at the "same thing," it is not the same thing at all. It is the strain of this appalling revelation that sets the students to work at last on the discipline of looking and leads them to discover that, by this discipline alone, a degree of reliability of perception becomes possible." [3]

Tracing perceptions to their sources leads, in one direction, to a still closer look at the objective case and, in the other, to an inquiry into the nature of the perceiver as an individual person and as a member of an organized, yet continuously changing, enterprise. The search leads into the intricate patterns by which the interpersonal context influences observation and thought, feelings that block one's view or others that open fresh avenues, confusions which lead to new departures, gentlemen's agreements not to learn about *that*, and so forth. The search leads into an inquiry of the nature of the group itself.

Historically, in fact, the really important changes in course procedures and subject matter have been to stimulate or, perhaps more accurately, to make room for a more explicit interest in group self-analysis. The major trend is described by Slater:

> [The course] . . . began as a practical course in industrial sociology and business administration, with cases used primarily to suggest alternative courses of action. Most of the cases concerned administrative problems in industrial situations, and little attention was given to the underlying theoretical issues. During a long period of transition, the action emphasis disappeared, the industrial cases were gradually eliminated and replaced by cases

---
[3] Perry, "The 'Human Relations' Course," *Journal of General Education*, p. 8.

dealing with family, college, and dating situations of more immediate concern to students, while the reading material came to deal
more with standard social science classics and to emphasize the
understanding of processes rather than problems of practical action. In the beginning there was no group self-analysis. . . . Such
analysis would not have been particularly meaningful, since all
interaction was channeled through the instructor. The result was
that, once a proficiency in case analysis was achieved, students
quickly lost interest in the situation, since the alternative of an
expansion in depth was closed to them. To remedy this defect,
more attention was focused on the group itself, and the role of the
instructor was modified to permit free interaction among group
numbers.[4]

With more freedom and the added responsibility of comprehending the here and now, the trend was away from the usual academic
seminar and toward training and therapy groups, particularly in the
exploration of issues such as dependency, commitment, intimacy,
rivalry, hostility toward authority, mutual affection, independence,
and separation. Often, the timing and nature of the instructor's interventions may seem indistinguishable from those of certain group
therapists. In spite of these similarities, and as implied previously,
the purpose, procedures, and products of the learning group are
quite distinct from those of the therapy group. The aim of the former
is learning, not personal help—although of course learning may be
helpful. Procedures are designed to gain insight, not to remove
symptoms—although of course insight may dissolve certain symptoms. Its scope is more limited than therapy in the sense that its
termination is decided by the academic calendar rather than by the
emotional state of its members. Moreover, grades are given; and although healthy students may often be evaluated highly, the evaluation is based upon skills rather than upon health. The role of a member is that of a student, not of a patient; the role of the leader is
that of a teacher, not of a healer.

As Slater has indicated, the course seeks to achieve a type of
learning through the "fusion of (1) the abstract principle, (2) the
concrete but objective instance, and (3) the subjectively and emotionally expressed instance."[5] Its use of the second of these dis-

[4] Philip E. Slater, "Displacement in Groups," in *The Planning of Change*,
eds. Warren G. Bennis, Kenneth D. Benne, and Robert Chin (New York:
Holt, Rinehart & Winston, Inc., 1961), p. 726.
[5] Slater, "Displacement in Groups," *Planning of Change*, p. 726.

tinguishes it from most training groups, and its focus upon learning distinguishes it from therapy groups.

Thirteen men and three women sign up for this section. Two of the sixteen are concentrators in social relations, one in mathematics, two in biochemistry, one in government, two in biology, one in economics, one in English, two in history, and one unreported. Two are on the football team, two are married, and two are Negro. Jewish, Catholic, and Protestant faiths are represented, as are the middle, lower-upper, and upper-upper social classes. Some are from New England, some are from the Midwest, others are from Texas, Florida, and California, and one is from South America. Ten sit at the central table, three sit back against the wall, and two of the women sit together.

The second session begins with the question, "What are our thoughts on the Michaelson case?"

One of the concentrators in social relations follows with a rather full précis on the Michaelson family, the thesis being that they were status-seekers through at least three generations. (The case, set in the house of a grandmother and grandfather, relates what happens when a son and his family move in. The backgrounds and the reactions to the move are presented under the authorship of the next-door neighbor.)

Shortly thereafter, the son Carl, his wife Eleanor, and Carl's mother Mrs. Michaelson, Sr., become special concerns to the group. Mrs. Michaelson is pictured as rigid (she divided the house into *ours* and *theirs* and locked away her best things), as impossible, and as dominant. Other comments suggest that she was insecure, that she needed someone to dominate, that if her son had said, "You are dominant and we're going to leave," she quickly would have replied, "Oh, no, don't, please don't. I love you and I need you"— "Meaning," a student suggests, "I need someone to control."

Mrs. Michaelson favored Henry over Carl, it is said.

At the end of the hour a student asks, "Can we take these cases at face value? How do we know the author is accurate? Might her opinions be just as colored as the opinions we're hearing here today?"

Thus their experience in analysis begins.

On leaving the session, one might recall that some of the students seemed to dislike Mrs. Michaelson, that some spoke of Carl as though he were their age rather than 50, that the children were rarely mentioned, and that two of the students argued over what is meant by dominant. Or, one may attempt more complete recall, setting down on paper a narrative report of the observed process during the hour. The content-analysis technique, called Sign Process Analysis and described in the next chapter, is designed to provide a record that is simply more selective and more systematic than such reports. In abstract, categorical terms, it records for each assertion the objects (who and what) referred to and the positive, negative, or neutral standards associated with the objects.

For example, during this first day, members make 517 assertions; the object most frequently referred to is one outside the group, a superior female (Mrs. Michaelson); next in rank, an external, subordinate male (Carl, Jr.); next, an external, subordinate female (Eleanor, Carl's wife and Mrs. Michaelson's daughter-in-law). Eighty-one per cent of the assertions referred to external objects and 17 per cent to objects and processes internal to the group (for example, "What was that you said?").

In this manner, Sign Process Analysis (SPA) shows that the discussion is oriented more toward things outside than toward objects inside the group. In addition, it shows that 18 per cent of the 517 assertions employ positive standards (for example, "She was fond of Henry," as above; or "I agree with what you said"); 46 per cent negative ("She needed someone to feel dominant over"; "I don't agree with what you said"); and, 36 per cent neutral ("Carl was older than Henry," or "How much more time do we have until the end of the hour?").

Taking objects and standards together, negative associations concentrate on Mrs. Michaelson (80 negative references) and on her relationship with her daughter-in-law. She is associated in a positive way, although infrequently, with her favorite son, Henry. Although many other breakdowns of the SPA data are possible, these few are reported here to indicate roughly what the method abstracts from the raw content. The classifications of objects and standards are sufficiently broad so that scores of one session may be added to or contrasted with scores of other sessions. Comparison with other sessions shows, for example, that this discussion is unusually high in it orientation to external objects, its references to superiors, and its preponderance of negative over positive associations.

It should be recognized that this group was chosen among many others for analysis not because it in some way represents more than others the universe of small groups. There is no thought that all small groups are similar to this one or that one can without effort generalize from this to others. On the other hand, there is the assumption that those lessons drawn from this group can improve group theory and in this indirect fashion affect the study of other groups. In this regard, a very special advantage of the type of group being analyzed is that part of its task is to understand its own process. Increasingly through the year, students openly report their intellectual and emotional experience as group members. Through discussion they examine ideas about what is going on in the group, what has happened in the past, what important changes have taken place, and what trends seem to be in effect. Members work toward an intellectual formulation which corresponds realistically to subjective experience and is at the same time comprehensible to others. In this sense, the work of the group is similar to the purpose of this book, and the author, being privy to the discussions, has learned from the group. He acknowledges with gratitude their contribution to the present formulation.

2

The Method
of Sign Process Analysis

Sign Process Analysis (SPA) is a disciplined way of recording and summarizing what is said in the course of group interaction. A remark is a set of signs and symbols which in ordinary circumstances has meaning for other members and, as a consequence, calls forth in their minds images, impressions, or ideas. As each statement is made, ideas associated with it are added to other already existing ones which, when taken together, constitute the culture of the group. The new statement contributes an *input* to that culture, and the input is recorded by SPA.

The method used in the present study distinguishes 396 types of input, a type being determined by the nature of the *object* (self, other, group, nation, artifact, and so forth) referred to and the *value standard* (positive, negative, or neutral) associated with the object. Each statement is scored in one of the 396 categories as it occurs in sequence, so that a summary shows the numerical frequency of the type of ideas presented. Theoretical grounds for the scorer's operation are given in the final section of this chapter. It should be mentioned here that classification is done without respect to the motives and intentions of the speaker and without regard to acceptance or rejection of the idea by other group members. Therefore, scores are of what was said as distinguished from motives and from what was meant to be said as well as from what was believed or finally agreed upon.

THE SCORING OPERATIONS

Basic Assumptions

To score inputs to group culture the scorer must assume the existence of that culture. He assumes that signs and symbols are taken by members to refer to roughly the same thing; that standards of what exists and what does not, of goodness and of badness, of desirability and of undesirability, of attraction and of repulsion—that these cognitive and evaluative standards exist within the culture to the extent that one or the other is implicated in every statement; and that he, as an observer, can interpret these standards and know how they are employed as members themselves define what it is that was said. As far as possible and with few exceptions, the observer uses the culture of the groups as his basis for scoring the input of a statement. He first interprets the meaning given to the statements by group members, and he then translates that meaning into his working set of categories.

Units

The communication process is taken piecemeal; that is, it is broken into units which correspond closely to the subject and predicate of the simple sentence. No more is needed for a statement to qualify as an input because, as stated above, inputs are classified according to the object referred to and the qualities associated with the object. "He is," for example, is taken as a unit. When either subject or predicate are implied in the context, the scorer makes the appropriate interpretation and scores the unit accordingly. "No," when interpreted to mean "I don't agree with you," constitutes a unit. Practically, the best guide for locating and distinguishing units is the existence of a predicate. In a given block of conversation the number of SPA units corresponds roughly to the number of predicates used or clearly implied.

Identification of Objects Referred To

Having separated comments into units, the scorer must then identify the nature of the object or objects being referred to, for which purpose he needs a general classification. The one used in the present study distinguishes objects according to their (1) locus, (2) sociological *status*, (3) *sex*, (4) *social* versus *nonsocial* nature, and (5) *individual* versus *collective* nature.

The classification is as follows:

Internal to the Interacting Group

1. Superior Male
2. Superior Female
3. Subordinate Male
4. Subordinate Female
5. Group Itself as a Collectivity

External to the Interacting Group

6. Superior Male
7. Superior Female
8. Subordinate Male
9. Subordinate Female
10. Collectivities (Various)
11. Nonsocial Environmental Objects

When acts initiated by a person are referred to, they are recorded in the class to which the person belongs. For example, "John's statement was wrong" is recorded in the same category one would record a reference to John.

Locus separates those objects internal to the interaction system from those external to it. In general, the distinction is straightforward. The inner includes the self, other members of the group, and acts and content of statements made by the self or others. It includes the group as a whole and the behavior of the group when it is referred to as the behavior of a collectivity. The distinction is made without regard to time, in the sense that what a group member did in the past or might do in the future is included as an internal object. On the other hand, it excludes nonsocial objects in the immediate situation such as microphones, tables, and chairs. It excludes an observer or other persons present who are not expected to interact with others and who are defined in sociological terms as being outside.

The second distinction is based upon relative sociological status. All social objects referred to in the course of one meeting are divided into one of two classes, superior or subordinate. In practice, the scorer lists all the objects referred to in the discussion and makes the division according to the most important and pervasive differentiation. For example, in the discussion of the family, the division is most often made between parents and children; in the discussion of a therapy group, between the therapist and group members; in an army unit, between officers and all other members of the unit. When the relationship is such that A is superior to B who is superior to C who is superior to D, the scorer must decide which difference in authority is sociologically most important.

The third distinction is between male and female, and the fourth is between social objects and nonsocial objects, all nonsocial objects also being classified as external. The final distinction is between

TABLE 1   SPA OBJECT MATRIX

Principal Object:	Principal Object Is Characterized:	Principal Object Is Related to Secondary Object Which Is:										
		Internal					External					
	1	2	3	4	5	6	7	8	9	10	11	12
		Superior Male	Superior Female	Subordinate Male	Subordinate Female	Group Itself	Superior Male	Superior Female	Subordinate Male	Subordinate Female	Collectivities (various)	Nonsocial Objects
Internal												
1. Superior Male												
2. Superior Female												
3. Subordinate Male	e			a					b			
4. Subordinate Female												
5. Group Itself	f											
External												
6. Superior Male												
7. Superior Female												
8. Subordinate Male				c					d			h
9. Subordinate Female												
10. Collectivities (various)												
11. Nonsocial objects	g											

social objects treated singly and those treated in collectivities. When the group as an entity is referred to, it is classified in category 5. When external units such as a family, the army, and so on are referred to, they are classified in category 10. Any and all objects referred to are classified in one of these 11 classes.

One-way and Two-way Units

The scorer finds that there are two types of units. The first consists of assertions that involve only one of the 11 classes of objects, for example, "*You* are well," "The *house* is white," "The *group* has met." The second type implicates more than one class, for example, "*I* talked with *him*," "*They* met *him*," "The *car* hit the *wall*." One-way units may be scored by a tally in that class, but two-way units usually involve a connection between classes of objects. To accommodate cross-classifications, an object matrix is devised. The matrix, shown as Table 1, has 11 classes of objects along both the rows and the columns so that any connection between objects and classes of objects may be indicated by a tally in the appropriate cell. A special column under the heading, "Principal Object Is Characterized," accommodates the one-way units. The following examples illustrate the location of objects by rows and columns:

	Row	Column
a. I agree with you. (when both are subordinate males)	3	4
b. I agree with him. (when both are subordinate males)	3	9
c. He agrees with me. (when both are subordinate males)	8	4
d. He agrees with him. (when both are subordinate males)	8	9
e. You are right. (when "you" is male)	3	1
f. We are wrong.	5	1
g. The house is red.	11	1
h. The boy hit the ball.	8	12

For most two-way units, the subject of the sentence is scored as the first, or principal, object in the appropriate *row* of the matrix, the second object being scored in the appropriate *column*. Consequently, the matrix scores reflect the directionality of assertions (largely action from first to second objects, from acting objects to acted upon objects). When (grammatically speaking) the passive rather than the active voice is used, the scorer simply reverses first and second object thereby maintaining the directionality.

In summary, each unit is scored in the object matrix. The location of this score indicates the class or classes of objects referred to in the statement. For any given unit there are 132 possibilities.

Depending upon the purpose of analysis, certain distinctions within the object matrix may be dropped. For example, the sex distinction is dropped in Table 2, which summarizes all entries made in the learning group during the eight-month period. It shows that, of the 34,000 entries made, over 22,000 [combining the internal subsums in the first column (86,328 and 4,307) with those in the fourth (5,435, 5,449, and 6,973)], or around 66 per cent referred to objects within the interaction situation and that a total of 8,035 [combining the external subsums in the first column (435, 1,342, and 2,245) with those in the last column (1,578, 1,816 and 619)], or around 23 per cent of the references, were to objects external to the interacting situation. In over 3,000 units, members in the group "acted upon" external objects (390, 884, and 1,947), whereas external objects "acted upon" members in only 247 instances (33, 57, and 161). From this very general summary we readily see that over the eight-month period members talked more about themselves than about anything else. Later charts show how the balance in this regard changes from the beginning to the end of the course. Table 3 presents the percentage distribution of scores throughout the matrix.

Positive, Negative, and Neutral Standards

The final operation of the scorer is to decide whether the cultural standard evoked by a statement is positive, negative, or neutral. In saying "The book is excellent," the speaker employs the evaluative dimension ranging, perhaps, from the very inferior to the very superior. As others hear his statement and "understand" it, they cannot help but call forth the evaluative dimension in their own minds. The question of the value of a book, for example, or more accurately, the question of evaluating a book is raised. Whether one agrees that the book is excellent or not, comprehension of the statement itself requires thinking in terms of "excellence." One feature of the input of the statement is to evoke this evaluative standard. SPA scores the nature of the standard that is evoked when a statement is made.

TABLE 2 SPA SUMMARY MATRIX: TOTAL RAW SCORES (Cells accommodate locus and status, not sex)

Principal Object:	Status	Principal Object Is Characterized:	Principal Object Is Related to Secondary Object Which Is:						
			INTERNAL			EXTERNAL			
			Superior	Subordinate	Subsum	Superior	Subordinate	Other	Subsum
INTERNAL									
Superior (Instructor, chairman)	+	0	3	112	115	0	0	1	1
	−	1	1	33	34	10	3	3	16
	0	11	3	1149	1152	7	4	55	66
Subordinate (Members)	+	86	424	4896	5320	89	23	277	389
	−	327	558	4857	5415	187	78	603	868
	0	4296	459	5362	5821	265	52	1564	1881
Subsum	+	86	427	5008	5435	89	23	278	390
	−	328	559	4890	5449	197	81	606	884
	0	4307	462	6511	6973	272	56	1619	1947
EXTERNAL									
Superior	+	166	4	5	9	143	278	76	497
	−	552	21	9	30	199	315	123	637
	0	778	29	43	72	44	92	70	206
Subordinate	+	205	7	6	13	351	430	178	959
	−	636	6	8	14	386	338	246	970
	0	1094	13	20	33	123	128	103	354
Other	+	64	0	11	11	14	45	63	122
	−	154	0	9	9	63	41	105	209
	0	373	0	56	56	5	17	37	59
Subsum	+	435	11	22	33	508	753	317	1578
	−	1342	27	26	53	648	694	474	1816
	0	2245	42	119	161	172	237	210	619

25

TABLE 3   SPA PERCENTAGE MATRIX (Cells accommodate locus and status, not sex)

Principal Object Is Related to Secondary Object Which Is:

Principal Object:	Principal Object Is Characterized:	INTERNAL — Superior	INTERNAL — Subordinate	INTERNAL — Subsum	EXTERNAL — Superior	EXTERNAL — Subordinate	EXTERNAL — Other	EXTERNAL — Subsum
INTERNAL								
Superior (Instructor, chairman)	+: .00 / -: .00 / 0: .03	+: .01 / -: .00 / 0: .01	+: .33 / -: .10 / 0: 3.37	+: .34 / -: .10 / 0: 3.38	+: .00 / -: .03 / 0: .02	+: .00 / -: .01 / 0: .01	+: .00 / -: .01 / 0: .16	+: .00 / -: .05 / 0: .19
Subordinate (Members)	+: .25 / -: .96 / 0: 12.60	+: 1.24 / -: 1.64 / 0: 1.35	+: 14.37 / -: 14.25 / 0: 15.73	+: 15.61 / -: 15.89 / 0: 17.08	+: .26 / -: .55 / 0: .78	+: .07 / -: .23 / 0: .15	+: .81 / -: 1.77 / 0: 4.59	+: 1.14 / -: 2.55 / 0: 5.52
Subsum	+: .25 / -: .96 / 0: 12.64	+: 1.25 / -: 1.64 / 0: 1.36	+: 14.69 / -: 14.35 / 0: 19.10	+: 15.95 / -: 15.99 / 0: 20.46	+: .26 / -: .58 / 0: .80	+: .07 / -: .24 / 0: .16	+: .82 / -: 1.78 / 0: 4.75	+: 1.14 / -: 2.59 / 0: 5.71
EXTERNAL								
Superior	+: .49 / -: 1.62 / 0: 2.28	+: .01 / -: .06 / 0: .08	+: .02 / -: .02 / 0: .13	+: .03 / -: .09 / 0: .21	+: .42 / -: .58 / 0: .13	+: .82 / -: .92 / 0: .27	+: .22 / -: .36 / 0: .20	+: 1.46 / -: 1.87 / 0: .60
Subordinate	+: .60 / -: 1.87 / 0: 3.21	+: .02 / -: .02 / 0: .04	+: .02 / -: .02 / 0: .06	+: .04 / -: .04 / 0: .10	+: 1.03 / -: 1.13 / 0: .36	+: 1.26 / -: .99 / 0: .38	+: .52 / -: .72 / 0: .30	+: 2.81 / -: 2.85 / 0: 1.04
Other	+: .19 / -: .45 / 0: 1.09	+: .00 / -: .00 / 0: .00	+: .03 / -: .03 / 0: .16	+: .03 / -: .03 / 0: .16	+: .04 / -: .18 / 0: .02	+: .13 / -: .12 / 0: .05	+: .18 / -: .31 / 0: .11	+: .36 / -: .61 / 0: .17
Subsum	+: 1.28 / -: 3.94 / 0: 6.59	+: .03 / -: .08 / 0: .12	+: .06 / -: .08 / 0: .35	+: .10 / -: .16 / 0: .47	+: 1.49 / -: 1.90 / 0: .50	+: 2.21 / -: 2.04 / 0: .70	+: .93 / -: 1.39 / 0: .62	+: 4.63 / -: 5.33 / 0: 1.82

Note: Due to rounding off, calculated percentages for the subsums are not always precisely the same as the sums of the percentages within the boxes.

26

Since most cultures possess a very large number of standards, it is necessary for the scorer to employ a simple but generally applicable classification. In SPA the scorer distinguishes among positive, negative, and neutral. He decides whether a given statement evokes the notions of (1) the good, the desirable, the loving, or (2) the bad, the undesirable, the destructive, or (3) others. Examples of inputs scored as positive are "This is the best I've done," "I prefer the one in red," "I agree," "She greeted him warmly," and "He has helped us"; examples of negative inputs are "It is no good," "I dislike it," "He broke all the rules," "He left in a fit of anger," and "They are anxious and afraid"; examples of neutral inputs are "It's rigged with stainless steel," "There are four minutes left," and "it was written in the first person." The first two categories accommodate evaluative standards, whereas the third accommodates the cognitive ones.

These simple categories with their emphasis upon the good-bad distinction are selected for SPA for several reasons: (1) the good-bad distinction seems to appear as universally in various cultures as does any other; (2) according to our experience in testing various classifications, it applies to a wider range of objects than do other standards, such as active-passive, and is therefore relatively independent from the nature of objects being referred to; and (3) scorers are able to employ it with good reliability. Its importance relative to other standards is confirmed by Osgood et al., who found that their factor I, good-bad, accounted for more variance than any other in their factor analysis of the meaning of concepts.[1]

In practice, two baselines are used for determining whether the standard is positive, negative, or neutral. The first, as we have indicated, is the set of values and norms of the society to which group members belong. Those which define the good, the desirable, and the loving, when signified by a statement made in the group, are classified as positive: an object is beautiful, a relationship is warm and trusting, a person is loyal to another, and so on. These are classified according to society's standards of beauty, trust, and loyalty. Those standards which define the bad, the undesirable, and the destructive, when signified by a statement made in the group, are classified as negative.

---

[1] Charles E. Osgood, George J. Suci, and Percy H. Tannenbaum, *The Measurement of Meaning* (Urbana: University of Illinois Press, 1957), pp. 31-75.

The second baseline consists of two ideal-type models: the love relationship and the destruction of one object by another. Having and seeking an object to love is scored as positive. Destroying or seeking to destroy someone or something is scored as negative. On those occasions when the norms of the society and the love relationship do not coincide, the classification is made in terms of the model of the love relationship; for example, brother-sister incest is scored as positive although it violates societal norms. Likewise, killing the enemy in war is scored as negative even though it is approved and rewarded by society. St. George's slaying of the dragon is scored as negative, whereas his being acclaimed a hero by the populace is scored as positive. The marriage of Oedipus to his mother is scored as positive, whereas his self-castigation for doing so is scored as negative. His banishment is scored as negative because the destruction of social relations and social ties is considered in the same light as is destruction of an object or a person.

Other baselines which might be confused with these two should be distinguished. Although recourse is made to the model of the love relationship and the model of destruction, it does not mean that positive, negative, and neutral characteristics are classified in terms of the psychic processes within the speaker. The needs of the speaker are not used in scoring SPA. "The mother loves the son," is scored positively, even though from another point of view the statement may be interpreted as an indication that the speaker wishes his mother loved him more, that he is being deprived of this love, and that he is, consequently, expressing a negative state of affairs. It is scored as positive, although from still another viewpoint it might be interpreted as a reference to the fact that he is gratified that his mother actually loves him. The positive score derives from the fact that reference is made to the love of one object by another. No effort is made to interpret the emotional state of the speaker—what gratifies him, what distresses him, his assets or his liabilities, his well-being, or his ill health. In this sense, scoring is done on the face value of the statement—face value being defined first by the societal standards and norms, and second by the pan-social models of the love relationship and of destruction.

In much the same way, no effort is made to interpret the significance of the statement for the ongoing stream of interaction within the group or its significance for the developing content of the culture. The issue as to whether the statement itself is appropriate or inappropriate, good or bad, regarding the progress of the group does not involve the scorer. It is true that if one member overtly approves a statement made by another member this approval would be scored as positive—scored as such, however, without concern that this approval is wise or unwise, appropriate or inappropriate, good or bad. In short, the categories of positive, negative, and neutral refer to content, not to an action's functional significance for the group.

Even though the SPA scorer is in this manner relieved of inferences regarding personality and certain characteristics of the social system, his task remains formidable; for with 132 cells in the object matrix and with the positive, negative, and neutral breakdown in each, he is presented with 396 possibilities in classifying each assertion.

The strategy of restricting the frame of reference to standards involved is a simple but important one. It is not yet known how motivational processes are dynamically related to cultural content, nor is it known how an act's function is associated with its content. These dynamic relations can be discerned only after data in each type of system are gathered in their own right. It is for this reason that SPA's distinction among positive, negative, and neutral is analytically independent of a statement's implications for the personality system of persons present, as well as independent from the progress of the immediate interaction situation. Connections among positive, negative, and neutral attributes on the various levels are matters for subsequent, separate, and distinct empirical investigation, an example being the study of the extent to which employment of negative cultural standards are associated with acts which take the group directly to its goal.

In summary, in scoring references as positive, negative, or neutral, two baselines are used. The first consists of the norms, values, and standards of the general society of which the group members are a part. The second baseline consists of the pan-societal, the pan-personal, and perhaps primal, models of the love relationship and of destruction. When the two baselines do not indicate the same classification, the second baseline takes precedence over the first.

Average SPA Scores
for a Session of the Case-analysis Group

Dividing the totals for the eight-month period by the number of sessions and omitting the sex distinction, Table 4 shows the average distribution of positive, negative, and neutral references throughout the object matrix. The number of positive references associated exclusively with internal objects is obtained by adding the sum of 1.00 in the first column to the sum of 79.93 in the internal summary column; similar additions are made for negative and neutral references. Eighty-one internal references are positive, 85 are negative, and 166 are neutral. The number of references exclusively to external objects is obtained by combining the external totals in the first column with those at the bottom of the last column. Thirty are positive, 46 are negative, and 42 are neutral. This single comparison indicates that the group is less neutral and more negative about outside objects than it is about internal objects. In a similar fashion, references made to persons in superior positions can be compared to those made to subordinates. Other comparisons can be made between the exchange of positive and negative expressions about high-status and low-status individuals. Continuing, one can compare the balance of positive and negative regarding high-status individuals within the group with the balance of those outside the group. Still further comparisons can be made with an uncompressed matrix between the signification of value standards regarding males and females, regarding males in superior positions, females in superior positions, males in superior positions within the group compared with those in a similar sociological position external to the group. Evaluations of objects in the outside world may be compared with evaluations of things internal to the group.

In recording what is talked about and the associated cultural standard, SPA provides a first approximation to the cultural content of group discussion. Just as signs (words, gestures, and so on) give hearers the notion of what the speaker is like, how he changes, and how he is apt to respond under special circumstances—as well as what he is talking about—SPA assumes that the analysis of signs will help us understand what groups are like.

TABLE 4 SPA MEAN MATRIX (Cells accommodate locus and status, not sex)

Principal Object Is Related to Secondary Object Which Is:

Principal Object: Is Characterized:	(Is Characterized)	INTERNAL			EXTERNAL			
		Superior	Subordinate	Subsum	Superior	Subordinate	Other	Subsum
INTERNAL								
Superior (Instructor, chairman)	+: .00 −: .01 0: .16	+: .04 −: .01 0: .04	+: 1.65 −: .48 0: 16.90	+: 1.69 −: .50 0: 16.94	+: .00 −: .15 0: .10	+: .00 −: .04 0: .06	+: .01 −: .04 0: .81	+: .01 −: .23 0: .97
Subordinate (Members)	+: 1.00 −: 4.81 0: 63.18	+: 6.24 −: 8.20 0: 6.75	+: 72.00 −: 71.43 0: 78.85	+: 78.23 −: 79.63 0: 85.60	+: 1.31 −: 2.75 0: 3.90	+: .34 −: 1.15 0: .76	+: 4.07 −: 8.87 0: 23.00	+: 5.72 −: 12.76 0: 27.66
Subsum	+: 1.00 −: 4.82 0: 63.34	+: 6.28 −: 8.22 0: 6.79	+: 73.65 −: 71.92 0: 95.75	+: 79.93 −: 80.14 0: 102.54	+: 1.31 −: 2.90 0: 4.00	+: .34 −: 1.19 0: .82	+: 4.08 −: 8.91 0: 23.81	+: 5.74 −: 13.00 0: 28.63
EXTERNAL								
Superior	+: 2.44 −: 8.12 0: 11.44	+: .06 −: .31 0: .43	+: .07 −: .13 0: .63	+: .13 −: .44 0: 1.06	+: 2.10 −: 2.93 0: .65	+: 4.09 −: 4.63 0: 1.35	+: 1.12 −: 1.81 0: 1.03	+: 7.31 −: 9.37 0: 3.03
Subordinate	+: 3.01 −: 9.35 0: 16.09	+: .10 −: .09 0: .19	+: .09 −: .12 0: .29	+: .19 −: .21 0: .48	+: 5.16 −: 5.68 0: 1.81	+: 6.32 −: 4.97 0: 1.88	+: 2.62 −: 3.62 0: 1.51	+: 14.10 −: 14.26 0: 5.20
Other	+: .94 −: 2.26 0: 5.48	+: .00 −: .00 0: .00	+: .16 −: .13 0: .82	+: .16 −: .13 0: .82	+: .21 −: .93 0: .07	+: .66 −: .60 0: .25	+: .93 −: 1.54 0: .54	+: 1.79 −: 3.07 0: .87
Subsum	+: 6.40 −: 19.74 0: 33.01	+: .16 −: .40 0: .62	+: .32 −: .38 0: 1.74	+: .48 −: .78 0: 2.36	+: 7.47 −: 9.53 0: 2.53	+: 11.07 −: 10.20 0: 3.48	+: 4.66 −: 6.97 0: 3.09	+: 23.20 −: 26.70 0: 9.10

Note: Due to rounding off, the means of the subsums are not always precisely the same as the sums of the percentages within the boxes.

31

RELIABILITY

The first of four reliability tests was made on written protocols of group discussions. Scoring was done by four trained persons who were divided into two pairs. The first pair of scorers compared tallies item by item; the second did likewise. In 269 units, one pair agreed on 230, regarding positive, negative, and neutral classifications. The other pair agreed on 206 out of 230. Using the Mosteller-Bush matching test, both z scores are far beyond the .001 level.[2]

In a second test, two persons scored a written protocol, and, as in the first, compared classifications item by item. The number of categories in this test was expanded from 3 (positive, negative, and neutral) to 102 (an object matrix of 34 cells, each with a further breakdown into positive, negative, and neutral, making 102 possible scores for any item). With an average of 554 units, classifications were identical for 409, or 74 per cent. Scores were clearly different on 105 items, whereas for 81 items one or the other of the scorers did not classify the unit. Thus, for the 514 units scored by both, 80 per cent of the scores were identical.

For most research purposes, indices are constructed from the total array of scores, each index being made up of a specified portion of the matrix. An illustration of the degree of agreement between two scorers on a series of such indices is given in Table 5, which summarizes scores of a selection of tape-recorded interaction. For ten indices the percentages are the same; for ten they differ by one per cent; for four they differ by two per cent. One notes, of course, that some indices incorporate others.

The third test was of total positive, negative, and neutral tallies in two other protocols. Each of four scorers was paired against each of the others, and comparisons were plotted on Mosteller-Tukey probability paper.[3] Out of the 36 instances of comparison, 18 were within 1 standard deviation and 32 within 1½ standard deviations.

The fourth and fifth tests were of object classification, one from

---

[2] Frederick Mosteller and Robert R. Bush, "Selected Quantitative Techniques," in *Handbook of Social Psychology*, ed. Gardner Lindzey (Reading, Mass.: Addison-Wesley Publishing Co., Inc., 1954), Chap. 8, pp. 307-11.

[3] Frederick Mosteller and John W. Tukey, "The Uses and Usefulness of Binomial Probability Paper," *Journal of the American Statistical Association*, XLIV (1949), 174-212.

TABLE 5   COMPARISON OF SPA INDICES OF TWO SCORERS

Index	Raw		Percentage*	
	First Scorer	Second Scorer	First Scorer	Second Scorer
1. Total Units	570	560		
2. Positive Units	106	115	.19	.21
3. Negative Units	116	101	.20	.18
4. Total References to Authority	164	170	.29	.30
5. Positive References to Authority	31	41	.05	.07
6. Negative References to Authority	52	44	.09	.08
7. Total References to Male Authority	0	0	.00	.00
8. Positive References to Male Authority	0	0	.00	.00
9. Negative References to Male Authority	0	0	.00	.00
10. Total References To Female Authority	164	170	.29	.30
11. Positive References to Female Authority	31	41	.05	.07
12. Negative References to Female Authority	52	44	.09	.08
13. Total References to Peers	331	331	.58	.59
14. Positive References to Peers	85	80	.15	.14
15. Negative References to Peers	56	48	.10	.09
16. Total References to Male Peers	246	249	.43	.44
17. Positive References to Male Peers	61	62	.11	.11
18. Negative References to Male Peers	47	42	.08	.08
19. Positive between Males	3	4	.01	.01
20. Negative between Males	2	2	.004	.004
21. Total References to Female Peers	154	157	.27	.28
22. Positive References to Female Peers	45	44	.08	.08
23. Negative References to Female Peers	35	29	.06	.05
24. Positive between Females	12	9	.02	.02
25. Negative between Females	5	4	.01	.01

Summary of Differences between Scorers:

	Number of Occurrences	Per Cent
Same Per Cent	10	.42
One Per Cent Difference.	10	.42
Two Per Cent Difference.	4	.17
Total	24	.99

Percentage obtained by using "Total Units" as a base.

33

a written protocol, one from tapes. In 24 instances of comparing general areas of matrix entries, 7 were within 1 standard deviation, 13 within 1½ standard deviations. Training and scoring written protocols improved results in the fourth test, where, out of 36 comparisons, 28 were within 1 standard deviation and 32 were within 1½ standard deviations.

Because of the interdependence of the categories (if it is not scored in one cell, it is scored in another), it is not possible to make a precise evaluation of the level of reliability evidenced in these tests, and thus it cannot be stated accurately that a sufficient level of reliability has been obtained for specified purposes. However, these tests do show that the method, as a standard set of operations, can be transmitted from person to person and that, when trained, the scorers use definitions and standards of classification which certainly approximate one another.

Eight persons are known to have learned and applied SPA. Experience shows that at least a month should be allowed for one scorer to teach the method to another, when teaching includes demonstration scoring from written and tape-recorded material, point-by-point discussion of the scoring manual, discussion of illustrative items, preliminary comparisons of over-all totals and, eventually, detailed comparisons of scores item by item.

THE THEORETICAL BASIS OF SPA

The purpose of the final section of this chapter is to state more precisely the theoretical frame of reference of SPA. The practical value of theoretical clarity is threefold: (1) it helps the scorer understand what he is and is not scoring; (2) it avoids confusion when data from SPA are compared with readings obtained by other techniques; and (3) it provides a basic position for resolving dilemmas which invariably arise when a systematic method is applied to ongoing group processes.

The general dimensions in content analysis of communication are summarized in Lazarsfeld's formula, "Who says what to whom in what context with what effect." [4] SPA is interested primarily in

---

[4] Paul F. Lazarsfeld, "Communication Research and the Social Psychologist," in *Current Trends in Social Psychology*, eds. Wayne Dennis *et al.* (Pittsburgh: University of Pittsburgh Press, 1948), pp. 218-19.

the first "what"; *what is said* is its subject matter. Of the many and often rich complexities of *what is said*, SPA, as indicated above, abstracts two: (1) what objects are talked about and (2) the class of cultural standard, whether positive, negative, or neutral, that is associated with the objects. This process of abstraction is based on a conception of social communication derived from sign theory and from sociological theory. A review of its essentials will clarify just what is scored by SPA.

Through the mechanism of reference, as suggested by Ogden and Richards[5] and subsequently developed by Morris,[6] conceptual distinctions are made among the word, the thought, the feeling, and the thing to which the remark refers. These distinctions effectively isolate the on-going stream of communicative events from other aspects of the social situation.

All methods that seek in some sense to understand the meaning of a statement are essentially subjective and, therefore, become immediately entangled in the ever retreating problem of what is meant by meaning. Morris' important contribution is to replace the vague and impossibly loose term of *meaning* by a refined set of concepts. He explicates both what he calls the sign and the conditions generally surrounding the sign. He postulates a sequence of behavior involved whenever an organism has a need, seeks its reduction, and reduces it. Instead of asking what a sign means, he asks, What role is played by the sign in this behavioral sequence? For example, is the sign telling where the desired object is? Does it indicate which is a better object? Does it indicate, even, which goal is the better one to pursue? In the following argument the distinctions of Morris are modified to apply to groups rather than to goal-seeking individuals. This shift from the individual setting to the group setting retains Morris' analytical distinction but requires a modification based upon this question: What role is played by the sign or by the communicative event in the group's development of its own culture?

Morris' technical explication of *sign* is as follows: "If something, A, controls behavior toward a goal in a way similar to (but not

[5] C. K. Ogden and I. A. Richards, *The Meaning of Meaning* (New York: Harcourt, Brace & World, Inc., 1938), pp. 1-13.

[6] Charles Morris, *Signs, Language and Behavior* (Englewood Cliffs, N. J.: Prentice-Hall, Inc., 1946). © 1946 by Prentice-Hall, Inc. Reprinted by permission of the publisher.

necessarily identical with) the way something else, B, would control behavior with respect to that goal in a situation in which it were observed, then A is a sign." [7] For example, the new traffic light supplanting the officer is, when flashing its signal to an on-coming motorist, a sign. Such behavior on the part of the motorist as driving, slowing, and perhaps stopping, is sign behavior. Morris continues, "If anything, A, is a preparatory stimulus which in the absence of stimulatory objects initiating response sequences of a certain behavior-family causes a disposition in some organism to respond under certain conditions by response-sequences of this behavior-family then A is a sign." [8]

Having explicated signs and sign behavior, Morris constructs a set of concepts to handle important aspects of the communicative situation that must be involved in one way or another in sign behavior. These concepts are as follows:

> Any organism for which something is a sign will be called an *interpreter*. The disposition in an interpreter to respond because of the sign by response-sequences of some behavior-family will be called an *interpretant*. Anything which would permit the completion of the response-sequences to which the interpreter is disposed because of a sign will be called a *denotatum* of the sign. A sign will be said to denote a denotatum. Those conditions which are such that whatever fulfills them is a denotatum will be called a *significatum* of the sign. [9]

It will be seen that two of these, the interpreter and the interpretant, relate to the organism in question; the other two, denotatum and significatum, refer to objects and conditions which are usually external to the organism and which are mediated by the sign vehicle.

The above terms are designed primarily as analytical tools for dealing with communicative phenomena as seen from the vantage point of the individual actor. What are the contributions and limitations of Morris' constructs in the analysis of social communication from the vantage point of the group as a whole?

Let us visualize a hypothetical situation of four interacting adults. With or without a joint purpose, they are in a state of intercom-

---

[7] Morris, *Signs,* p. 7.
[8] Morris, *Signs,* p. 10.
[9] Morris, *Signs,* p. 17.

munication (of some undefined minimum degree), a state mediated by signs and symbols. How would Morris' concepts apply? There are, first of all, four interpreters. For any given sign, there are four different interpretants; there are four different significata, for significatum is anchored to conditions related to individual and idiosyncratic goals. If one chooses to record significata, one must record four scores for every sign introduced into the system. This criterion naturally generates into N number of scores, where N equals the number of members in the group, and is at once a serious limitation.

There is another not so obvious complication. From the vantage point of any one actor, the other three members are potential denotata and significata as well as interpreters; and, insofar as dispositions of group members may be talked about, interpretants become potential significata and in some respects potential denotata. The flexibility of everyday symbolic manipulation renders a simple situational shift from the individual goal-seeking pattern to the group an extremely complicated matter. If the scheme is to be retained as it is and if it is to be used as a means of estimating group processes, it requires, to begin with, enough information to interpret personality dispositions for all persons in the group and, then, inferences as to common significata and noncommon significata. Furthermore, this estimating must be done under constantly changing conditions. Clearly, at the point of detecting dispositions, or patterns of dispositions, and of determining the relationships among these subsystems of dispositions, the matter has gone beyond both the tools of semiotics and the practicalities of systematic scoring.

However, in the shift from the individual to the group situation, it is important to note that the one thing that has not increased in complication in any manner whatsoever is the sign vehicle itself: for one person, one sign; for the four persons, one sign. What has become complex is the many views taken of the single sign. This distinction between what remains the same and what increases in complexity as we add members to the group constitutes an important theoretical development on the part of the semiotician. *In an increasingly complicated situation he has succeeded in isolating the ontological constant.* Beginning with this constant, SPA modifies the concepts of Morris so that they are useful in analyzing group phenomena. The theoretical and practical complications that arise as one shifts from the individual to the group require more abstract concepts, such as those found in sociology and in particular in the action theory of Parsons, Shils, and others.[10] These authors distinguish three systems: the personality system, composed of needs and motives and their organizational superstructure; the social system, composed chiefly of the mutual or complimentary expectations of interaction sequences; and the value system, composed of the collection and organization of standards of what things are, what things are desirable, and what things should be (where "things" include, among many items, behavior of the self and of others).[11] Any one of these systems may be studied in their own right, but all are involved in any social interaction.

An essential feature in the two constructs of the social and value systems, and one that makes the degree of abstraction possible, is the shared nature of expectations of behavior and of value standards. This feature, which is of central importance in our discussion, enables a scorer to make one scoring entry for every sign vehicle regardless of the number of people in the group.

Let us note the importance of the differences in the three types of systems mentioned above. If one were concerned with personality, one would ask, What dispositions are aroused by this event? what dispositions in each of the personality systems included in the interaction situation? There are at least N number of questions and N number of answers, where N equals the number of members. In the terminology of Morris, the connection within this system framework concerns sign and interpretants; in the terminology of Parsons and Shils, the connection concerns action and need-dispositions of actors. There is no essential difference between the two approaches when personality systems are the central issue.

The difference appears when our concern shifts to the social system. Returning to our hypothetical group of four members, let us assume that it is a "system," that is, that members either share a common goal and know they do or that they are committed to a

---

[10] Talcott Parsons, Edward A. Shils, and James Olds, "Values, Motives and Systems of Action," in *Toward a General Theory of Action*, eds. Parsons, Shils, *et al.* (Cambridge, Mass.: Harvard University Press, 1951), pp. 47-275.

[11] Parsons, Shils, and Olds, *Toward a General Theory*, pp. 3-27.

traditional pattern of group procedures. Let us assume further that one of the members suggests a certain course of action for the group as a whole. We may then ask, What significance does this suggestion have for the movement toward or away from the group goal or for the traditional pattern of behavior? Framed in this manner, the question permits a single answer, regardless of the number of members, the structure of the group, and so forth, and, consequently, introduces an enormous simplification into the analysis of group process. The advantage of this viewpoint, which enables the scorer to give one score, and only one score, to each unit, is taken by Bales in his Interaction Process Analysis.[12]

Furthermore, if one's interest is in the value system, or more generally, in the culture of the group, one may ask, What shared standard of definition is employed in the statement? What shared evaluative standard is employed? Again, the assumption of the existence of a culture within a group enables the scorer to make one entry for each sign vehicle, regardless of the number of people in the group.

Since one asks about something shared rather than about an individual's disposition, the following modification of Morris' concepts is appropriate:

1. Call the modification of his interpreter, *definer*.
2. Call the term corresponding to his interpretant, *definition*.
3. Call the term corresponding to his denotatum, *standard denotatum*.
4. Likewise, call the term corresponding to his significatum, *standard significatum*.

These concepts represent the shift from personal needs, motives, and ideas to those definitions and ideas that constitute group standards.

By the introduction of these changes, the definition of *standard denotatum* becomes: anything that would permit the satisfactory identification, confirmation, or verification of the definition stimulated because of the sign. Correspondingly, the definition of *stand-*

---

[12] Robert F. Bales, *Interaction Process Analysis* (Reading, Mass.: Addison-Wesley Publishing Co., Inc., 1950).

ard significatum is: those conditions which are such that whatever fulfills them is a standard denotatum.

What, one might ask, *are* the conditions which, if fulfilled, permit identification, confirmation, and verification of a definition? There can be no identification, confirmation, or verification without established cognitive standards that not only operate for a single person over various time periods, but also are shared simultaneously by a number of persons. For example, the minimum conditions for the verification of the statement and corresponding definition of "the house is green" include cognitive standards covering what a "house" is, what "green" is, and what "is" is. Without such standards the statement is "meaningless." *Thus, within this context, that which is signified by a sign corresponds exactly to that which Parsons and Shils call cognitive standards.* To signify is to evoke a cognitive standard. Patterns of signification correspond to patterns of those cognitive standards utilized. The same is true for evaluative standards of reference where, however, both definition and evaluation are signified.

According to this schema, there may be N number of definers or evaluators and N number of definitions or evaluations; but just as there is only one sign, there is only one standard significatum— only one set of conditions corresponding to the appropriate cultural standards. Supported by the working assumption that a state of communication exists within the group, the modification makes one score for each sign that occurs both possible and legitimate.

The scorer using SPA employs this modified conceptual framework. He makes no assumption about the motivation of the members of the group: He is not interested in what a person wants, only in what he says. He makes no assumption about the interaction goal of the group or the relationship between the event and this goal. He *does*, however, assume the existence of cultural standards and their part in every statement made.

If one accepts for the group as well as for the individual a basic sequence beginning with a shared definition of the situation and followed by its evaluation, which is in turn followed by decision and execution of the decision, the assumption of shared cognitive and evaluative standards is, in an important way, less inclusive than assumptions about each personality system and about the action system as a whole. The former assumption is made prior to and independent of the question of individual goals and prior to and independent of the question of the purpose or patterned direction of the group as a whole. Its elementary nature comes from the claim only that certain shared standards are evoked.

3

The Chronology
of Negative and Positive Scores

The first purpose of this chapter is to record the session-by-session readings in negative and positive categories in order that other instructors and group leaders may use them as a basis for comparison. Its second purpose is to gain a first approximation of the connections between content categories and dynamic processes of the group. To this second end, major peaks and troughs are examined in the light of what else is known to be happening in the group at those periods. Happenings may be historical events, such as the presence of a stranger or the absence of the instructor, or they may refer to the subject matter being discussed, in which case they may be identifiable through a more refined breakdown of the content than is reported in summary charts. The problem, for example, is to understand more fully the occasions on which an unusually high negative reading occurs. Was anything out of the ordinary happening? What was on the agenda? What did the group discuss? Can a comparison of the various occasions on which negative peaks occur suggest the group properties and processes that are manifest by negative scores? This preliminary analysis of negative and positive categories leads to another level of analysis (in the next chapter) where day-to-day readings are smoothed into trends.

THE NEGATIVE

The six peaks in negative expressions at points marked A, C, D, H, J, and N are shown on Chart 1. The first two are associated with references to authority figures external to the group. As noted on page 17, the first discussion focused in a negative fashion on Mrs. Michaelson, Sr., who was excluding her children and grandchildren from her area of the house. After this initial peak, the curve decreases steadily to one of the low points of the year (when readings by Fromm, Piaget, and Freud are on the agenda), then increases to C, on November 2 during a consideration of the Thomas case. Written by a chemistry major, this case reports an outbreak during vacation of a long-term conflict between her mother and father, both of whom were trained as research scientists. Forty per cent of the references are to authority figures (the parents) who are involved in three-fourths of the negative references. Thus, the first two negative peaks are occasioned by discussions about authorities outside the group.

The second and third peaks are associated, in part, with the more immediate authority, the instructor. After dropping prior to the hour examination and the holiday, the curve again peaks when the instructor forgets the projector for showing a film. It peaks again at H upon his return after an absence. Between the peaks, a series of events take place which are probably critical to the life of the group.

On November 30, a day on which the instructor has suggested consideration of the outside readings, a male student, early in the hour, asks for special permission to make a comment. Silence falls, whereupon, he goes to the blackboard, lists four headings, sketches a fairly complex diagram, and proceeds with a well-organized lecture on neuron connections and their significance for understanding human behavior. The instructor has moved from the top of the desk where he usually sits to a nearby chair, which he turns to face the board. As the lecture comes to an end, silence again falls over the group.

During the following session, it is suggested that the group would do better without the instructor. This suggestion could be a test— a test of the idea voiced by several that he doesn't make any difference to the group. Another member thought that his absence could test the independence of the group. Another asked why "the instruc-

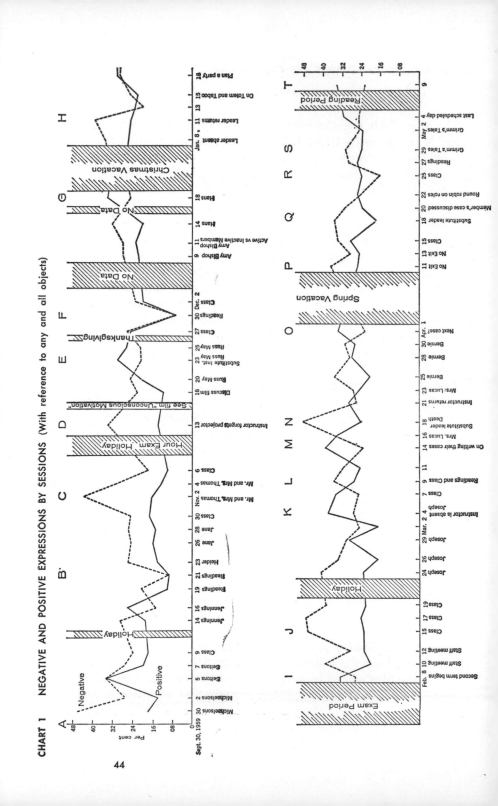

CHART 1   NEGATIVE AND POSITIVE EXPRESSIONS BY SESSIONS (With reference to any and all objects)

44

The *Michaelson Family* case may be found in Hugh Cabot and Joseph A. Kahl, *Human Relations*, Vol. II (Cambridge, Mass.: Harvard University Press, 1953), 14.

One of the themes of *The Seiton Family*, discussed on October 5 and 7, and also in Cabot and Kahl, p. 50, is why members of the family are unable to express their feelings to one another.

The case of *Allen Jennings* (October 14 and 16) reports a college freshman's weekend visit at home. Allen interprets a decision by his parents that he may go to New York for a weekend as a step toward independence.

Readings (October 19 and 21) include selections from Eric Fromm's *Escape from Freedom*, J. Piaget's *Language and Thought of the Child*, S. Freud's "Three Contributions to the Theory of Sex," and E. G. Schachtel's "On Memory and Childhood Amnesia."

The Fritz Heider film (October 28) is a short, abstract "cartoon" presenting the interrelated movements of geometric figures. It may be used as a projective motion picture.

Jane resembles her mother and her sister-in-law, Mary, who has moved into the family home (October 26 and 28).

Mr. and Mrs. Thomas (November 2 and 4) concerns another home visit by a college student who reports discussions about the careers of her father, her mother, and herself.

In the film *Unconscious Motivation* (November 16), a fictitious childhood experience is introduced to two students under hypnosis. Subsequently, they interpret their own responses to projective stimuli as they try to piece together details of the experience.

Russ May writes his version of an incomplete love affair.

Readings on November 30 include selections from T. Leary's *Interpersonal Diagnosis of Personality*, Freud's "Psycho-

pathology of Everyday Life," and Hayakawa's *Language in Thought and Action*.

Amy Bishop recalls the death of her father and the perplexing reactions of her family and herself which surround it.

Hans refers to Freud's "Analysis of a Phobia in a Five-year-old Boy."

Readings during the later part of the first term include further selections from Freud; D. W. Baruch's *One Little Boy*; G. Bateson *et al.*, "Toward a Theory of Schizophrenia"; selections from B. Malinowski's *Sex and Repression in Savage Society*; and L. J. Henderson's "Procedure in a Science," in Cabot and Kahl, noted above.

Staff Meeting (February 10, 12) is set on a farm being used as a religious retreat, managed by a woman who takes St. Francis as her model.

Joseph (February 24) is the biblical story.

Readings for the spring term introduce small group processes, social structures, ethnic boundaries, intergroup feelings, and religious and symbolic processes. Most frequently mentioned in class are F. Redl, "Group Emotion and Leadership," in Hare, Bales, and Borgatta, *Small Groups*, pp. 71-87; W. G. Bennis and H. A. Shepard, "A Theory of Group Development," in Bennis, Benne, and Chin, *The Planning of Change*; Lillian Smith, *Killers of the Dream*; O. Rank, *The Myth of the Birth of the Hero*; and H. M. McLuhan, *The Mechanical Bride*.

After the death of her husband, *Mrs. Lucas* (March 16) moved to America. The case concerns her relations with her daughters, as adults.

Bernie (March 25) is a senior in college. He writes this case as a son, a Jew, and a senior.

No Exit (April 11) is the Sartre play.

Grimm's Tales refers to three versions of the fairy tale sometimes called "The Seven Swans."

tor sits way up on top of the desk instead of down with the rest of humanity?" Others joined in a game of "how can we get Mills off the desk."

Chart 1 shows that the year's lowest negative reading was taken during the student's lecture and that the frequencies increase fairly regularly to a peak at H. A breakdown according to superior-subordinate references (internal and external) shows that negative references to the instructor increase steadily from F through H, reaching their peak for the year at H. Though negative references among members parallel this increase, their peak is later, at J.

The second term begins with two strangers present. Having been told by the instructor that no transfers are permitted nor are new members admitted, the class in due time asks them to account for themselves. "Did Dr. Mills tell you to come?" "Did he let you come in?" "No," they say, "but what kind of group is this anyway?" "What's been going on all fall?" "What's so great about it that you don't want us in it?" Sensing some vulnerability, the outsiders press their attack. Several leading members defend the course, its purpose, its procedures, ending with the comment, "But how can you understand. You have to be *in* it to know what I mean—it's a group that's different." From this point, negative references increase to J, reaching the second highest and most sustained peak of the year.

This peak is associated with the pitting of one member against the group. With the biblical story of *Joseph* as the case on the agenda for February 2, a male member, much as though he were a stranger, turns on the group in an all-out attack: "The group is not a group; it has gotten nowhere. Members are not insightful but stupid. They can't see what is going on in the cases—one can't believe the writers of cases anyway—and if they could, they wouldn't be able to prove their point satisfactorily. How can you tell what's good or bad in a course like this? How can one grade an examination on *Totem and Taboo* or on *The Bible?* All I hear in these discussions is hogwash—just a lot of nothing. A course where the teacher says nothing, does nothing, *is* nothing." For most of three sessions he attacks. Gradually, the group discussion shifts to Joseph and his brothers. Negative expressions subside, then rise to their last substantial peak at N, when, again, a substitute instructor is present. A minor trough occurs at O, just before spring vacation;

and a major one at R, during a general recapitulation of the group's experience during the year.

In summary, negative peaks during the fall term are associated with the issue of authority: the first two with parents in cases, the next two with the instructor himself. The deepest trough occurs when a student assumes a traditional instructor's role. Expulsion of authority is the theme of the rise to the final peak.

Expulsion or inclusion of a person as a member is the theme of the rise to the first spring peak. Negative expressions refer both to peers and to authority figures. The final peak is reached on a day when a substitute represents the instructor.

Thus, five out of six major peaks are associated in some manner with the issue of authority, and the sixth involves both peers and authority. The earlier ones are in respect to external authority, the subsequent ones with the instructor himself.

These observations suggest that unusually high readings in the negative category are involved in some manner with the authority issue and with what the authority stands for. We shall examine the matter further in the next chapter, after tracing the curve of positive expressions.

THE POSITIVE

Six out of nine major peaks in positive expressions occur on the day before separation (for example, before Christmas vacation) or during separation (for example, when the instructor is absent).

The first peak is at E, when case discussion under a substitute instructor is about the unsuccessful love affair of *Russ May;* references are chiefly external. The second is just before Christmas vacation; the third on January 18, is at the last meeting before the mid-year examination—a session taken by the group to plan a gala social affair. The fourth is at K, on March 4. With the instructor snowbound, a member organizes the session, purchases a tape from a nearby record shop, sets the tape recorder, and announces that "We can meet as usual and present the tape to Dr. Mills." The fifth is before spring vacation.

The final positive peak associated with separation is at the last session. A discussion of whether to meet or not had come up in the previous session because scheduled classes were over and meetings during reading period were optional. Some felt too busy. Others favored one more class. One wanted to meet, as he put it, "to get this group organized." Eight, including the four more active members, attend the last session. Talk is strained, and few themes are followed through. Members look vacant as they sit far apart around the table. "Why was it we did so poorly?" "Why couldn't we really ever make a group decision?" "Shall we have a reunion next fall on the bank of The Charles?" When at the end of the hour the bell tolls, one of the leaders looks slowly around, saying, "I just can't believe this is the end."

On this last day, 93 per cent of the comments are internal; only 7 per cent refer to outside subjects, such as The Charles. The group is far more "introspective" than it was on the first day. The members are more positive as well: 34 per cent compared with 18 per cent. Moreover, they conceive of the group differently; during the first meeting there were 11 references to the group as a collectivity (*our* section, and so on), whereas during the last, there are 385.

The three other positive peaks are distributed throughout the year: (1) On October 5, when the group discusses the *Seitons*— "a close knit family" kept within bounds by a father who prohibits expressions of feelings; (2) on the first day of spring term, when the group defends itself against the strangers' challenge; and (3) on March 14, at M, when members talk over their cases under preparation.

These observations suggest an association of some sort between unusually high positive readings and dispersal of the group, or with anticipation of being dispersed. A more refined analysis is necessary before one can specify the conditions under which such an association holds, and indeed just what, more precisely, the association means. Some further suggestions are made when, in the next chapter, we consider the question of affection as one of the group's major issues.

4

Group Issues
and Data Trends

On the critical side, it can be argued that data like those reported in Chapter 3 are so subject to misinterpretation that they are, at best, fruitless. It is too easy, in the first place, to extract more from a scoring scheme than one puts into it. One scores manifest content, for example, and later talks of group feeling; or, for another, one scores only the active verbal part of the group but infers by implication to the group as a whole, as though the silent processes—which are the majority—do not exist. Second, without an experimental design or a battery of independent readings, any association between a datum and a selected group characteristic is fortuitous and arbitrary. Such associations are convincing only after other sources of variance are known and can be evaluated. In addition to these limitations, there is the likelihood that groups are so subject to change that even though, when immature, they manifest a state of affairs in one manner they may, when mature, manifest the condition in an entirely different manner (for example, early anger and later pleasure at the instructor's absence may manifest a similar process). This tendency would mean, of course, that inferences depending upon comparisons of peaks and troughs would be dissociated from what is actually going on in the group.

This conservative argument sounds a necessary warning, points to pitfalls that should be avoided, and casts such analyses into a healthy state of tentativeness, but it hardly serves as a practical program for developing a more useful theory. Moreover, there is a danger of taking it too seriously and thereby overlooking the fact that some conceptual schemes for groups and portions of theories about group dynamics do exist. Using their experience as observers or as practitioners in groups, various students of groups have formulated what to them are the major issues and the characteristic developmental trends of groups confronting these issues. Though neither Bion's[1] formulation, nor Bennis and Shepard's,[2] nor Foulkes and Anthony's,[3] nor Shutz',[4] nor Parsons, Bales, and Shils'[5] pretend to be fully comprehensive, they do provide a working theoretical base for selecting those issues of group structure and process to which systematic content analysis might fruitfully be related.

Drawing from these writers and from experience in groups like the one under study, in this chapter we formulate the central issues —issues no such learning group could easily avoid—trace possible ways of resolving them, and then examine the observed developmental trends in categories of content analysis as shown by SPA. To the extent that the formulation coincides with experiences of other observers and to the extent that the trends approach expectations derived from the formulation, additional grounds exist to suggest the group processes that are manifest in content data.

ENTERING NEW TERRITORY

On encounter, the group does not know what to make of itself, the instructor, or the course in general. Neither constitution nor blueprint exists. Any guides are negative ones: It is soon clear that

---

[1] W. R. Bion, *Experiences in Groups* (New York: Basic Books, Inc., 1961), pp. 41-75.

[2] W. J. Bennis and H. A. Shepard, "A Theory of Group Development, *"Human Relations,* IX (1956), 415-37.

[3] S. H. Foulkes and E. J. Anthony, *Group Psychotherapy* (London: Penguin Books, Ltd., 1957).

[4] W. C. Schutz, *FIRO: A Three-dimensional Theory of Interpersonal Behavior* (New York: Holt, Rinehart & Winston, Inc., 1958).

[5] Talcott Parsons, Robert F. Bales, and Edward A. Shils, *Working Papers in the Theory of Action* (New York: The Free Press of Glencoe, Inc., 1953).

neither the teacher's role, the materials, nor the role of student corresponds to other courses. In the beginning, a member does not know how far he should go in expressing his feelings about characters in the cases or about what someone else in the class says. His expectations are not clear on how open discussion is to be, on what is appropriate or inappropriate to say, or even on what case analysis consists of. With this much uncertainty, it is inadvisable to be too frank, too open. The more he shows his hand the more vulnerable he becomes. He tends to let others proceed, for in new territory he can get lost and hurt.

Nonetheless, a student characteristically moves into the first case with a directness, a seriousness, and an intensity that belies uncertainty. Mrs. Michaelson is dominant, rigid, unfeeling, a poor kind of mother to have; Carl, her son, is weak, indecisive, and still a young boy. Others join in, and value judgments come more freely than does corroborating evidence. Different stands are taken, and a student remarks, "How can there be so many different opinions— we all read the same case?"

Interventions by the instructor are designed to help differentiate facts in the case from value judgments about them, Mrs. Michaelson's feelings from one's feelings about her, and in general, emotional currents in the case from emotional currents in the group itself. As speakers see themselves in what they say and as the group discusses what is going on in the here and now, the earlier naiveté gives way to self-consciousness. "We can't talk about the case without saying something about ourselves." "The cases are to get us to reveal ourselves." "We're all just projecting—we see what we want to see in the case." "I have revealed more of myself than I intended to." As though having overextended itself, the group closes up and retreats.

Retrenchment, however, is counteracted by other pressures. Readings shift from the issue of dependence-independence to concepts of moral absolutes and autonomy, then to unconscious processes and their manifestations. On November 16, the class views a film called *Unconscious Motivation* which is, among other things, an effective comment on the relief of anxiety through comprehension of unconscious feelings. Meanwhile, the instructor encourages and protects those who openly express their feelings about the cases or about the class. He interprets unconscious processes associated with general group issues so that, by experiencing clarification of group issues, members may gain confidence in making such interpretations themselves.

Consequently, members are subject to cross pressures: on the one side, a need to retrench for security reasons; on the other, a desire to go deeper and farther for the experience of clarification. The issue is whether or not persons will enter the role of student, committing themselves to explore wherever that goal might take them. Can members carve out roles that are appropriate for the task and conducive to learning or are roles to be defensive devices?

If our aim is to formulate precisely the process of learning and the amount that is learned, content-analysis data cannot help very much. If, on the other hand, the modest aim is to detect entry into or departure from a more general role, then the point may be made that one does not enter and commit oneself to the role of student of these cases and the group without analyzing and expressing positive and negative values and feelings. They are a necessary part of the role. Although the limits are unknown, it is probable that unusually high neutrality means being out of the role and that substantial increase in neutrality (with other things being equal) indicates a departure from the role. However, low frequencies do not necessarily mean that one is in the role, for such evaluations and feelings are implicated in other roles. Low frequencies mean only that being in the role is a *possibility*.

The trend of neutral comments is presented in Chart 2, where points represent three-session moving averages.

Retrenchment is apparent in the increase of neutral comments from the first to the tenth session. Subsequent swings down and up reflect approach and withdrawal associated with the desirability and danger of confronting more emotionally charged material. December 2, however, proves to be the breaking point of the entire year, for from this peak the average declines sharply, never to rise again above a ceiling. Variations occur before and after the breaking point, but the two levels are distinct. The change seems irreversible, except for the last few sessions as the life of the group comes to an end.

Although norms cannot be judged from this type of data alone,

CHART 2   TOTAL NEUTRAL EXPRESSIONS
(With reference to any and all objects)

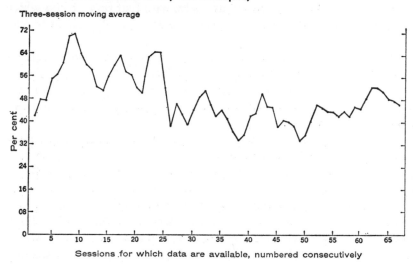

Sessions for which data are available, numbered consecutively

it is not unusual in groups of this sort for inhibition, intellectualization, evasion, and neutrality in general to be defined as deviant
from the learner's role: One is expected not to retrench. The later
ceiling may be a normative ceiling. If so, it became formulated and
established around the first week in December.

It is on December 2, as noted previously, that the group openly
confronts the instructor with the proposal that he leave or that he
at least move from atop the desk to a lower-level chair. Though
revolts such as this take various forms, they have been noted as a
regular occurrence in training groups[6] and on one level may correspond, as Slater suggests[7] in referring to classes such as this one,
to the totemic processes discussed by Freud.[8] Though the revolt's
full consequences for the group are probably not fully understood,

[6] Bennis and Shepard, "A Theory of Group Development," *Human Relations*, IX.
[7] Philip E. Slater, "Totemic Processes in Groups" (Brandeis University: Unpublished manuscript).
[8] Sigmund Freud, *Totem and Taboo* (New York: W. W. Norton & Co., Inc,
1952).

it has been suggested elsewhere[9] that the aggressive confrontation either facilitates, or is an overt manifestation of, identification with the person in charge, or more precisely, with that part of him which is relevant to the collectivity, in this case with learning about human behavior.

Content analysis shows that the decrease in neutrality follows soon after the revolt. Although, as we have said, low neutrality is not evidence in itself that members have entered, or are in, the learner's role, the data indicate such a possibility after, but not before, the revolt.

In summary, for a group investigating new material by new means, a central issue is whether or not they will create a working role which incorporates the functions necessary for accomplishing the task and, associated with this, the question of the extent to which members will commit themselves to the task and to that role. Case analysis demands exploration of personal values and feelings, often on the preconscious level. The student enters territory which for many seems new, uncharted, and possibly dangerous. Conflict is between retrenchment and exploration.

If the trend of neutral comments is interpreted in these terms, the initial increase, subsequent oscillation, and eventual decline to a lower level correspond, in order, to the retrenchment (following initial naiveté and growing self-consciousness), conflict between retrenchment and exploration, and, eventually, sustained engagement with affective material. As expected from previous clinical analysis, sustained engagement follows a revolt against the instructor. Whether members enter completely into the student's role cannot be determined by these data alone.

CONFRONTING THE HERE AND NOW

The instructor announces on the first day, it will be remembered, that part of the group's work is to observe, analyze, and understand its own process, much as it would a case. Subsequently, he suggests that an hour be devoted to a discussion of what has been going on in the group. At first, members are reluctant to confront the here and now and, instead, find themselves returning to the cases, refer-

---

[9] Theodore M. Mills, "A Sociological Interpretation of Freud's *Group Psychology and the Analysis of the Ego*" (Unpublished manuscript, 1959).

ring to other groups, or legislating for the future. The instructor assists their confrontation of themselves by drawing attention to the way current events, such as the absence of a member, a change in seating, or a bid for group leadership find themselves expressed in analysis of the cases.

These interventions, when successful, introduce two levels of observation and interpretation: (1) what comments express about the here and now, and (2) what they say about the case or other external contexts. To the role requirement mentioned above, that the students deal with affective material, can be added the demand that they observe and interpret their own process of observing and interpreting.

Chart 3 shows trends in the locus of what is talked about throughout the year. Internal references (I, you, what you said or did, the group, and so on) are plotted with a solid line; external references

CHART 3   LOCUS OF REFERENCE:
INTERNAL ALONE COMPARED WITH EXTERNAL ALONE

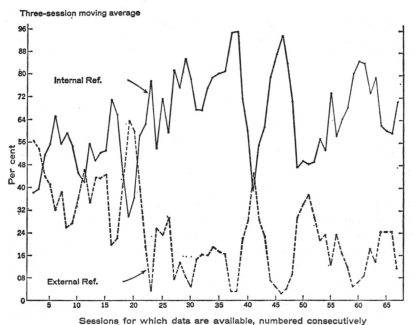

Three-session moving average

Per cent

Internal Ref.

External Ref.

Sessions for which data are available, numbered consecutively

(Mrs. Michaelson, Piaget, the other section, and so on) are plotted with a broken line. The unmistakable trend is toward internal matters. The group maintains about a 50-50 balance up to and around November 27; the internal emphasis then increases to a peak near the 37th session—a week after the beginning of the second term. Discussion of cases such as *Joseph and His Brothers, Mrs. Lucas, Bernie,* and *Grimm's Tales* accounts for peaks in external reference but does not counteract in any sustained manner the group's preoccupation with itself.

It is interesting that the end of the oscillation between external and internal and the beginning of internal preoccupation coincides with the "revolt" and the radical decrease in neutrality. Though concern with the here and now is again not conclusive evidence that active members have entered the student's role, more than before they discuss in positive and negative terms what the group itself is doing.

CONFUSION, ANGER, AND DISSATISFACTION

From their inception, training and therapy groups are under stress. The case-analysis group is not only without the usual protections surrounding academic students but the members' defenses as such come under scrutiny. Some students, possibly sensing this, leave after a few sessions.

The first major source of strain is associated with the instructor. In fantasy at its more primitive level, he is omniscient and omnipotent; in actuality, he refuses to give instruction. Responsibility for inquiry and formulation is placed on the student, yet his observation and interpretation is neither approved nor disapproved by the instructor. No rating scale appears. The student has no authoritative baseline for evaluating the worth of what is said. Because the instructor withholds just those things other teachers are paid to give, the student is angered because his comments and acts seem emptied of significance. "I came to see you because in most of my courses so far I have gotten 'A's' and I couldn't tell in class just what is required for an 'A' in this course."

The group issue, as Bennis and Shepard define it, is whether or not there will be created an independent role, as distinguished from rebellion against the authority and from dependence upon him.

A second source of strain is associated with a member's peers. If in a class the instructor does not talk to him, and he cannot easily talk to the instructor, he must turn, however reluctantly, to his peers. Aside from violating an ancient schoolroom taboo, talk with his peer in such a setting subverses the competitor role. The more open the give and take, the less advantage he has over the other. Moreover, closeness grants a right to be judged and an obligation to judge—which means not only that the seat of judgment is shifted from instructor to the group but that competitors are expected to evaluate one another. A group member comes under the control of his peers. If he produces nothing, he is ignored; on the other hand, "You have to be very careful not to do anything too good; the better it is, the more of a prat-boy you become." Feeling abandoned by the instructor and turned over to the group, members become resentful and touchy. In such a delicate position, they may either ignore their fellows and perform for the instructor (in a sense, talking to one another out of the side of the mouth), or they may gradually create mutually collaborative roles.

Intellectual uncertainties intensify the dissatisfaction. It is not clear what constitutes good and adequate case analysis. Though suggestive, the cases seem to lack enough concrete data to warrant substantial conclusions. The student becomes aware that speakers see in the case what they want to see, yet this observation cannot be proven. Often his clearest reaction to the case is emotional and seems hardly expressible in an academic setting. Comments tend to add to the confusion rather than to clarify matters. Often contradictory observations are made, each seeming valid but neither being demonstrable. Moreover, no analysis is complete. "Are we going to leave all cases as we left *Allen Jennings?* You know, up in the air. Was he dependent or independent? Can you tell us so we can go on?"

The fourth strain is the extremely difficult and seemingly endless task the class is asked to undertake in comprehending its own process. Who anywhere has succeeded in observing, formulating, and documenting the processes of groups? Interpretations must be interpreted, and these, in turn, must be analyzed, and so on, endlessly. Events accumulate at too great a speed to be unraveled. Some members, like instructors and clinical analysts, may still be working on this unfinished task.

In short, students are given a new responsibility in working together on tasks that are exceedingly difficult, both intellectually and emotionally. They experience confusion, dissatisfaction, and anger. Negative readings in the content data provide some estimate of how these strains are manifested and handled.

However, before turning to the negative trends themselves, it is advisable to consider the various factors which contribute to the high and low negative readings and to see how the combination of factors through time might lead to changes in over-all readings.

High negative readings may be accounted for, first, by the case material. Discussion of conflicting cases, such as *The Michaelsons, Mr. and Mrs. Thomas,* and *Joseph,* for example, produces high negative frequencies which, at least on their manifest level, are apart from what is going on in the group. Second, the rising reservoir of feelings associated with accumulating, unresolved strain, as outlined above, when and if expressed is likely to be in negative form. How to separate these two factors is not at all obvious. Although the scoring scheme distinguishes external references (to cases, for example) from internal references, symbolic manipulation allows a member to express an internal strain in an external guise so as to confound, for content classification, the true source of the negative reading. This problem is discussed in Chapter 6; for the moment we simply acknowledge these two sources. A third source for high negative readings (particularly when sustained) is the constructive, instrumental consequences of working through conflicting viewpoints and positions. Hot debate may lead to clarification; or, challenging the group may lead to its acceptance. The engagement in one realistic conflict after the other, each new move being reinforced by the success of the former, may account for an increase in negative comments as well as for sustained high readings. A fourth factor is the balance between fear of counterattack and the probability of being protected in expressing oneself openly. In this regard, a member of a neighboring section imagined the group as a zoo. "The animals there behind their cages, pacing up and down. And there is the keeper." Only after realistic, local tests can one know how strong, how compassionate, or how punitive the instructor may be and how tolerant or merciless members may be. Assurance of protection and experience in the constructive consequences of conflict encourage the expression of a larger proportion of the reservoir of negative feelings, thereby contributing to higher over-all readings.

In the other direction, some factors tend to depress negative scores. The first is positive or neutral content in substantive material, examples being *Russ May* and the outside readings. Second, there are the inhibitions arising from both internalized norms against seeing and expressing negative matters and an uncontentious strategy in safeguarding one's position in the group. The third factor is a combination of the dual consequences of having expressed negative feelings in the past: One consequence is catharsis and the other is the actual resolution of issues underlying original strain. For example, as the point of contention between member and instructor is negotiated and partially resolved, catharsis and success tend to reduce negative readings.

None of these factors is assumed to be constant through the life history of a group. The agenda, for example, determines case content; and the strains associated with the instructor, peers, and the difficulty of the case analysis are assumed to increase during the first period of the course. Inhibitory factors increase early. On the other hand, the sense of assurance of being protected increases more slowly and only after adequate tests. The constructive consequences of working through the issues of strain are experienced still much later.

The hypothetical order in which the various factors reach their maximum are as follows: (1) inhibition, (2) issues of strain, (3) assurance of protection, and (4) resolution of issues of strain. Consequently, we can expect through the year an over-all increase, then a decrease, in the frequency of negative expressions.

Chart 4 presents the three-session moving average percentage of negative expressions. Though an apparent cyclical pattern exists, it is around *a general trend, which increases to a peak near the 37th session and then decreases to the end of the year*. Both peaks and troughs within the cycles follow, by and large, the rise and decline.

Though not charted, a breakdown into the internal and external references shows (1) that the latter actually *decrease* from the beginning to the 37th session, (2) that the peaks at the initial and 14th sessions are composed principally of external references, and

CHART 4   TOTAL NEGATIVE EXPRESSIONS
            (With reference to any and all objects)

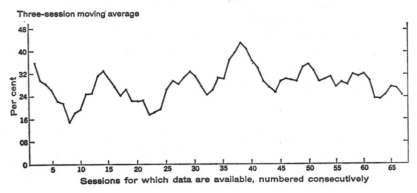

Three-session moving average

Sessions for which data are available, numbered consecutively

(3) that, following the 37th session, internally oriented negative expressions trend downward while those associated with external objects exhibit no general trend. Consequently, *the rise and fall of internally oriented negative expressions is more distinct than indicated in Chart 4.*

Further breakdowns show that (1) as noted above, negative expressions regarding the instructor rise around the first week of December (the time of the revolt), *increase* to a peak prior to the mid-year examination, then *decrease,* generally, to the end of the year; (2) negative expressions among members of the group *rise* to a peak during the all-out attack by a member around the 37th session, then trend *downward.* Thus, both types *increase,* then *decrease.* The peak associated with the instructor occurs a month before the peak of those referring to group members.

In summary, we interpret the increase to the 37th session as resulting from (1) an increasing reservoir of actual strain, (2) a decrease in inhibitory factors, and (3) growing assurance that the expression of the negative will be protected. We interpret the decrease after the 37th session as a result of the resolution (relatively speaking) of certain underlying issues of contention and, consequently, a lesser reservoir of strain. The decrease in negative references to authority following the 30th session and the decrease in similar references to peers following the 37th session indicate a reduction of strain associated with these two issues in that order.

AFFECTION

A fifth area of strain arises from the libidinal forces in the group —a student's admiration and love for his teacher and his fellow students. Strain exists because the taboo against acknowledging and expressing these feelings is perhaps the strongest taboo of all. He may call a relationship within a case "good" or "bad," but he hesitates to identify fully with the person in those relationships who is loving. He may agree or disagree with his fellow students. He may rate and rank them along an academic or some other scale, but he hesitates to show his affection for them as persons. Ultimately, in fantasy, intimacy is a dyadic and private affair, which makes it an illusive thing to see in a case being discussed publicly. Also, intimacy can be divisive to a group seeking an integrity of its own and attempting to describe boundaries between itself and the external world.

Grounded in the sociology of a young group, the taboo hides tenderness and love when it appears in a case and veils its existence and inhibits its expression among group members. It is reinforced by fears of rejection, uncertainties over boundless involvement, and costs of unlimited responsibility.

Only when the group forms its boundaries, obtains its identity, is there something local to love which is nondyadic. As the group itself becomes an object to which members can commit themselves, the taboo on tenderness lifts; for, once the group is formed, affection is felt toward one who is a joint member. The identity of the group affords a reassuring boundary which places limits upon rejection, involvement, and responsibility. The fantasy of the disruptive withdrawing, narcissistic dyad is translated into a communal process.[10]

Creating group identity takes time. The taboo does not. Consequently, one should expect initial depression of the curve of positive expressions, giving way gradually to an increase as the group forms itself and the taboo is attenuated.

The moving averages of positive expressions are presented in Chart 5. Though subject to cyclical peaks and troughs, *the trend for the year is upward.* The initial decrease parallels the early decline

---

[10] Philip E. Slater, "On Social Regression," *American Sociological Review,* XXVIII (1963), 339-64.

CHART 5   POSITIVE EXPRESSIONS

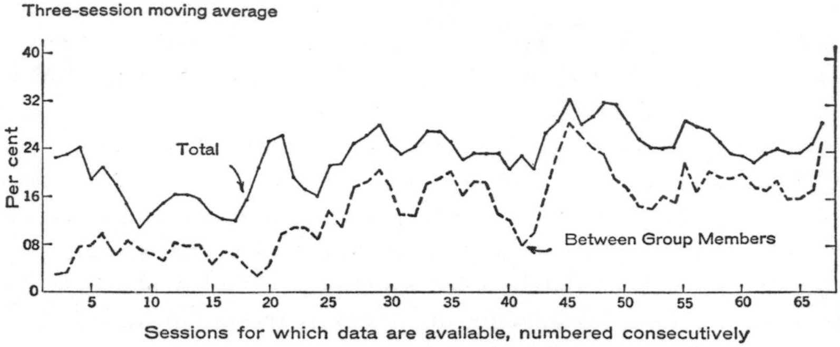

Three-session moving average

Sessions for which data are available, numbered consecutively

in negative expressions during retrenchment. The peak for the year comes early in the second term (*after* the peak in negative expressions), and a rise occurs as the group disperses at the end of the year.

Those positive expressions which refer exclusively to group members are indicated by the dotted curve on Chart 5. These are made up of such statements as, "That's a good idea," "Now, we are saying something!" "The group means a lot to me," and so forth. In their frequency, one finds three distinct plateaus: the first from the beginning to the 21st session, the second to around the 43rd, and the third following the peak around the 45th. Beginning low, positive expressions increase in two steps. The first appreciable rise follows "the revolt"; the second follows the discussion of the case of *Joseph*. The theme accompanying the first is expulsion of authority; the theme of the second, expulsion by the brothers of a favorite son. In both cases the rise to a higher positive plateau follows conflict over basic group issues.

Two interpretations, each needing further corroborating evidence, may be suggested to explain the connection between overt conflict and higher position plateaus. The first is that members gain confidence in the group because it weathers a storm. In spite of the revolt, the leader remains. In spite of the student's attack, both he and the group remain. Conflict may disturb the group, but if it stands the test, members acquire new confidence. This reassurance is expressed indirectly in their discussion of the cases and in their interpersonal behavior.

The second interpretation, which is in part an elaboration on the first, is that new role relations are being created and accepted in the course of overt conflict. The revolt marks the transition from dependence upon the leader as the final authority to a challenge of his position, and, indirectly, a challenge of the authority upon which any position in the group is based. In similar fashion, conflict over the case of *Joseph* marks the transition from a competitive, destructive relation among members to one that permits, yet contains, the expression of strong differences. In the first conflict, relations change from *follower–leader* to *student–instructor;* in the second from *competitor* to co-worker or *collaborator.* The creation and acceptance of these new role relations reconstitutes the group. More nearly than before it is a learning group, and as roles are redefined in these terms, as the object of one's affection becomes defined as co-worker rather than as total person, as boundaries to the give and take of affection become drawn, the taboo on expressing affection subsides. Affection among co-workers is not strictly a dyadic affair but communal and, consequently, legitimate. It is thus more readily expressed.

SUMMARY

Borrowing from clinical and other observers, we have formulated in this section central issues for learning groups. Is orientation to the instructor to be dependent, rebellious, detached, or independent? Is orientation to a member's peers to be competitive, condescending, contentious, or collaborative? Are the realities in the cases and in the group to be used, ignored, or respected and understood? Are feelings of affection to find a legitimate and satisfactory channel of expression? Is creative work to be done? These issues are a basis— but by no means the only one—for interpreting major trends in content-analysis data.

Through the separate analysis of neutral expressions, of internal versus external references, of negative and of positive expressions, two events stand out as especially important in the transformation of the group: (1) the "revolt" against the instructor, after which neutral references decrease, internal references increase, negative references to authority increase, and positive expressions rise to a new plateau; and (2) the student's attack on the entire enterprise (combined with the discussion of the case of *Joseph*), after which negative expressions decrease, positive ones again rise to a somewhat higher plateau, and there are no substantial changes in other content categories.

5

Toward a Conception
of the Life Cycle of Groups

One of the more deeply perplexing and taxing experiences for the person entering a learning group like the one being reported is the speed at which events, in kaleidoscopic confusion, appear. Often it is expressed in images of "jungle noises," "being at sea," "horses off in all directions," "being shot at from all quarters," "a mess, a mess, a mess," and so on. "We have never, don't now, and will never know what is going on, and if someone says he can untangle it, that just makes it worse." One might imagine similar images going through the mind of a totally naive person at his first baseball game. Events appear strangely confused, disordered, and unpredictable. Only after one conceives *the game* do these events take their meaningful and enjoyable place in an ordered pattern. Only then do certain events become significant, central, and exciting —though perhaps still unpredictable.

The experienced group leader, or the well-trained observer, has at least an implicit conception of what goes on in men's minds and something of what transpires in groups. By deciphering the multi-faceted meaning of comments, he discerns more order and patterns than can the initiate. In fact, a number of teachers, therapists, observers, and social scientists have sensed the existence of certain structures and of ordered change in these structures. Currently, there is a variety of formulations which attempt to make clear the phases, developmental sequences, cycles, or the like through which groups tend to go. The authors of these schemes perhaps share the assumption that a "game"—albeit ingenious and complicated—is being played and that random-like events will become more ordered, more meaningful, more significant once the "game" is conceived, formulated, and understood.

Quite appropriately, these preliminary conceptions of systems in change vary according to the type of group and its goal and according to the professional role or theoretical interest of their authors. For example, for short-term, intellectual, problem-solving groups, Bales conceives of phases in terms of the intellectual processes of orientation, evaluation, and decision, these being paralleled by an increase in socioemotional issues.[1] For groups training normal adults in human relations, Thelen and Dickerman formulate four phases: (1) members' attempt to establish their customary place in the power hierarchy; (2) leader's rejection of this hierarchy and of authoritarian goals, resulting in frustration and conflict; (3) cohesion and complacency; harmony at all costs; (4) combination of group-centeredness and serious efforts at "work."[2] Phases in his therapy groups are formulated by Mann as (1) hostility serving to bind members through mutuality of feelings, (2) anxiety about closeness, (3) personal mutual analysis, and (4) personal mutual synthesis.[3] Bennis has revised the two-phase (six subphase) conception of group development of Bennis and Shepard into three phases: (1) oral-inclusion, (2) anal-responsibility, and (3) phallic-intimacy.[4] Aiming at a more abstract level, Parsons, Bales, and Shils suggest an ever-ascending spiral created by four-stage cycles, the stages being addressed to the problems of (1) adaptation, (2) goal reduc-

[1] Robert F. Bales and F. L. Strodtbeck, "Phases in Group Problem Solving," *Journal of Abnormal and Social Psychology*, XLVI (1951), 485-95.

[2] H. Thelen and W. Dickerman, "The Growth of a Group," *Educational Leadership*, VI (1949), 300-16. In these references on group development, I am indebted to the work of Warren G. Bennis in a working paper on group development (1957a) and in some problems and research gaps in group development (1957b), Group Research Project, Massachusetts Mental Health Center.

[3] James Mann, "Group Therapy with Adults," *American Journal of Orthopsychiatry*, XXIII (1953), 332-37.

[4] Bennis, 1957a.

tion, (3) integration, and (4) emotional expression and maintenance of patterns;[5] more recently Parsons has presented a more refined conception of the cycle.[6]

Perhaps these examples are enough to suggest the enormous utility of a clearly conceived, comprehensive model of the major sequences in group structure and process. Enough is known from observation and experience to say that groups are inherently complex systems with a vast number of variables changing simultaneously. Valuable as knowledge of the correlation between two or three of them might be, there remains the question of the place of one correlation within a set of many; and insightful though the comprehensive clinical analysis of the motivation of one event, or of the motivational system of one member, might be, there remains the question of its ramifications in an interdependent system. Though current models may be open to justifiable criticism because of bias and gaps, as they are improved they can help the practitioner place a single event or variable within a multivariate context and relate the here and now both to the past and to the future, much as the fan does with his fairly complex model of the game of baseball.

The discussion of the life cycle of learning groups presented on pages 70-80 was prompted, first, by the desire to understand more clearly how readings in content analysis are associated with major changes in the group and, second, by the need, in my opinion, to emphasize certain processes which have been observed in learning groups but which have not found their way into current conceptions of phases, cycles, and developmental sequences. The first of these is the process of forming indigenous norms, that is, of giving up preconceived normative notions, of creating normlessness, of experimenting with and selecting new ones, and of refashioning them through experience. One part of this process, of course, is the creation and modification of the full set of role relations within the group. In most current formulations, these processes, which are

---

[5] Talcott Parsons, Robert F. Bales, Edward A. Shils, *Working Papers in the Theory of Action* (New York: The Free Press of Glencoe, Inc., 1953), pp. 163-269.

[6] Talcott Parsons, "Pattern Variables Revisited," *American Sociological Review*, XXV (August 1960), 467-83. See also Talcott Parsons, "The Point of View of the Author," in *The Social Theories of Talcott Parsons*, ed. Max Black (Englewood Cliffs, N.J.: Prentice-Hall, Inc., 1961), pp. 311-63.

difficult to tie down empirically, are excluded. Problem-solving sequences such as those of Bales, for example, deal with frequencies of types of behavior in an extranormative sense. Unincorporated within the hypothesis are questions of what members believe the behavior should be and whether or not it coincides with contractual relations within the group. Moreover, although sequences in therapy groups may trace the rise and fall of anxiety, rarely is there consideration of the anxiety-reducing function of entering into a contract with one's "rival" or with one's "master." Changes in norms and changes in motivational states are intimately related. For these reasons, the discussion of the life cycle emphasizes normative processes.

The second emphasis is upon *partial* consummation. Until much more is understood about human behavior, and insofar as members of learning groups realize what is *not* known by them or by anyone else, there is an incompleteness to their experience. They may have started on an enterprise, but by no means do many groups feel that they have gained total wisdom. In terms of initial and even subsequent expectations, members ordinarily feel that they have fallen short of the group goal. Consummation in learning groups is partial and fragmentary, as it may be in therapy groups. In spite of this limitation, however, current formulations, without an important exception, portray in the way persons and the group change an eventual climb to an ideal peak. The picture is of members who express themselves freely and discern accurately while they listen, comprehend, and achieve consensual validation—this, while the group becomes integrated. Some characteristic final phases illustrate the point: *The Working Group* (Bach),[7] *Combination of Group-Centeredness and Serious Efforts at "Work"* (Thelen and Dickerman),[8] *Focus of Responsibility Becomes Fixed in Group* (Gordon),[9] *Personal Mutual Synthesis* (Mann),[10] *Productive Collaboration* (Semrad and Arsenian),[11] *Integrative* (Coffey and Leary).[12]

---

[7] George R. Bach, *Intensive Group Psychotherapy* (New York: The Ronald Press Company, 1954), pp. 268-93.

[8] Thelen and Dickerman, "The Growth of a Group," *Educational Leadership*, VI.

[9] Thomas Gordon, *Group-centered Leadership* (New York: Houghton-Mifflin Company, 1955), Chap. 10.

[10] Mann, "Group Therapy with Adults," *Journal of Orthopsychiatry*, XXIII.

[11] Elvin V. Semrad and John Arsenian, "The Use of Group Processes in Teaching Group Dynamics," in *The Planning of Change*, eds. Warren G.

Whether the formulations refer to groups far more successful than those observed by the author, or whether the formulation expresses what should happen rather than what in fact does happen, remains to be learned from further rigorous empirical examination. Until such time, the discussion of the life cycle notes some of the effects partial consummation has had upon the learning groups observed by the author.

The third emphasis is upon the fact that most learning groups terminate. Anticipating this death and handling its reality is an important issue to those who commit themselves to the group. Though separation anxiety and the process of termination are familiar to many therapists and trainers, they have not gained an important place in the formulations of group development, phase sequences, and so forth. Why this is so is probably not a simple matter. It may be associated with the desire to think only about positive aspects at the end of the group's life; it may result from the pervasive and culturally patterned denial of death in our society; or it may be rooted in an underlying sociological assumption that while persons die, institutions and societies live on. In any case, no formulation, to my knowledge, adequately accommodates group mortality. Some, in fact, would seem to require fundamental modification to make room for processes of dissolution, liquidation, and separation.

Emphasis upon norms, imperfect consummation, and dissolution should not be interpreted as an exclusion of other issues and processes which have already been summarized in developmental sequences. The following discussion, in fact, assumes, is indebted to, and builds upon the perceptive and stimulating conceptions of Bennis and Shepard, Semrad and Arsenian, Parsons, Bales, and Shils, and seeks by its special emphasis to add its contribution to a comprehensive formulation. At the same time, the emphases are based upon the belief that the realities of group process are such that a comprehensive model must be in terms of a life cycle—group formation and group dissolution—rather than simply a progressive development toward some implicitly desired state.

Bennis, Kenneth D. Benne, and Robert Chin (New York: Holt, Rinehart & Winston, Inc., 1961), pp. 737-43.

[12] H. S. Coffey et al., "Community Service and Social Research," *Journal of Social Issues*, VI (1950), 25-37.

ISSUES AND ACTIVITIES
IN THE LIFE CYCLE OF LEARNING GROUPS

There are five principal periods: (1) the encounter, (2) testing boundaries and modeling roles, (3) negotiating an indigenous normative system, (4) production, and (5) separation. For each period, the central issues, the predominant activity, and the group properties which emerge as a consequence are briefly suggested. The discussion does not attempt to include all areas, issues, or mechanisms, for example, certain sources of personal anxiety and their defenses, the progress of role differentiation and the probable structures, the more complex patterns of symbolic manipulation, and the process of member and group clarification. Instead, it presents a likely course in terms of selected variables. Moreover, it does not attempt to follow through the fate of groups which vary from this particular course nor to specify the fate of those which become arrested at particular points along the way.

The Encounter

ISSUES

The first issue is whether or not a group will actually materialize. Will a sufficient number of persons return and continue to attend? Second, and if they do, to what degree will the arrangements and procedures that are worked out be conducive to accomplishing the announced aim.

For a prospective member, the first issue is: Do I want to belong to the group in view of what the experience might demand and what it might give? Second, am I capable of being a member? Am I, for example, able to see what I don't want to see, to do what I prefer not to do, to be appraised by those I don't want to judge me? Looking far ahead, will what I can give be valued by others?

ACTIVITIES

Among characteristic responses to these issues are the following:

Naive activism.   Based upon preconceptions of group discussion, of human behavior, of one's role in similar contexts, and supported by the hope that these conceptions handle most contingencies, members rush into the task.

Disillusionment. Due to the almost universal inadequacy of the preconceptions, to a growing awareness that to embrace a task is not the same as performing it, and to an uncertainty arising from the value differences among members, disillusionment occurs.

Retrenchment. As a consequence of disillusionment, members withdraw from the more complicated areas of the task and suppress their more personal thoughts.

EMERGENT PROPERTIES

If the enterprise continues, the following new components or states are likely to exist.

Within the group, there is a state of anomie. Preconceived notions about what should be felt, said, and done and about the roles of member and instructor are found inadequate and inappropriate and, hence, must be given up. Since there is no indication from any authoritative source concerning what notions might or should take their place, anomie exists.

Persons arrange a new contract with themselves, as it were. They enter an arrangement whereby they agree to give more to the group than they receive immediately, and they leave themselves more than usually vulnerable, intellectually and emotionally.

In short, the group emerges from the encounter with certain members making long-term investments and committing themselves to a state of anomie.

Testing Boundaries and Modeling Roles

ISSUES

A central issue of a group in such a state is to determine the scope of anomie. Of the previous ideas about what the group should be and about what should be done, how many are to be given up, how many modified, how many retained? How extensive is the uncertainty? how deep the involvement? how threatening the process? A second issue is the character of the arrangement that might replace anomie. What constitutes a learning group? What is involved in creating a productive and satisfying arrangement?

For a group member, the central issue is: Can I try new stances, new roles, when chance of success is low and risk of failure is high?

Can I go ahead without authoritative approval and disapproval as a guide? To what extent dare I risk being called a fool?

ACTIVITIES

With a distant goal, but with no normative guides from any source, one likely set of responses is (1) to retest pragmatically the limits of preconceived ideas, and (2) to model new behavioral roles so that their scope, their effectiveness, and their appropriateness may be experienced and judged by members. Boundary-testing and role-modeling are likely to be oriented to the following issues:

Commitment. The importance of the group to oneself may be tested by being absent; the importance of one's own performance, by giving one's very best ideas or by remaining silent; the worth of the performance of others, by overt challenge or by silent critique. The strength of others' commitment is tested and gauged.

Authority. The apparent discrepancy between the expected and the announced role of the instructor is tested by attempts to manipulate him into the more conventional active, directive, appraising, and nurturant role, or by taking his role, or by organizing a substitute authority structure. Tests are made of the members' fantasy of him as omnipotent and omniscient and of them, in relationship to him, as ignorant and impotent. Unbelieving, they test above all the instructor's assertion that he will not legislate for them and give to them a new system. In the course of these attempts, the roles modeled include the rebellious, the recalcitrant, the doctor's helper, the usurper, the silent supporter, and the independent student.

Intimacy. Tests are made for an equitable, comfortable distance between members, often by approaching too close and pulling too far away. Similar tests are made of (1) the limits of self-revelation and of what one can tolerate seeing in others, (2) the range of tolerance of similarities and of differences among members, (3) the lasting power of one's initial likes and dislikes and of one's admiration and devaluation of others, and (4) the solidarity of subgroups which might offer security. Modeled roles may include the cold and the detached, the intimate and the anaclitic, the open and the personal, the fellow student and the colleague. Testing and modeling are oriented to the definition of acceptable boundaries of particularistic, diffuse, and affective interpersonal relations.

Work. What more exactly is involved in "understanding human behavior?" The process of seeking knowledge is tested by trying to let the facts speak for themselves, by simply accepting or rejecting a case instead of understanding it, by trying to explain a case from the application of a single theory or set of concepts, and by attempting to exhaust the material from an analysis of only the conscious level. Testing all the way, the group members move facing backward into work. Tests seek those circumstances which give absolute certainty to one's interpretation. Tests explore how infinite the regression is when one attempts to understand another's attempt to understand someone's attempt to report events. Modeled roles are those of jurist, academician, romanticist, scientist, poet, philosopher, and artist. Since the issue of exploring what the group might or wants to become is critical, discussion of external matters, such as cases or events of community and nation, become screen discussions within which the exploration of the group's future continues. Issues of commitment and authority are explored and tested in this substitute context. For this reason, there is ambiguity concerning what a speaker is referring to, and there is no distinction between the feelings about external objects and about internal ones.

In summary, processes during this second phase are devoted to testing boundaries and modeling possibilities in respect to *personal commitment, authority, intimacy,* and *work.* Exploration permeates the boundary between the group and the external situation so that these distinctions are not clear.

EMERGENT PROPERTIES

The following new components, or states, are likely to exist as residues of experimentation.

Since testing boundaries, modeling roles, and formulating conclusions from these activities *are* part of the process of learning about human behavior, there exists—though perhaps still unformulated—a notion of what it takes to be productive and a feeling of satisfaction in having begun to learn. Therefore, there vaguely exists a sense of goal-direction, a sense that is based pragmatically upon the group's experience.

Consequently, there also exist grounds not only for selecting those issues which are relevant to the goal but for evaluating the possible alternative ways of handling issues. There exist, in other words, both motivation and a rudimentary set of values to guide the formation of a new normative system.

Negotiating an Indigenous Normative System

ISSUES

Having dropped certain preconceptions, displayed a range of possibilities, experienced progress in learning, intellectually and emotionally, and gained a sense of goal direction, the group's central issue is to legislate an enabling set of norms. How are values and preferences to be formulated into ideas concerning what should and should not be done, and concerning what sorts of interpersonal relations should prevail?

For a group member, the central issues are: Can I perform the student role in this group and still be the kind of person I am and want to be? Is the role which is preferred both creative and compatible with my needs and capacities?

ACTIVITIES

With a rudimentary but pragmatically based sense of the legitimate and the preferred, the group is likely to negotiate a new set of norms and to select agents who sanction and control on behalf of these norms. Whereas earlier roles of experimenter and explorer were modeled, now roles of sanctioner and controller are modeled. Negotiations focus upon the following familiar issues:

Commitment. Attempts are made to establish the criteria for group membership. The right of members to consume time to make a personal point, the right of silent members to receive without giving, the right of absent members to return without paying a price, these rights are all challenged. The uncommitted portions of the group and of persons are sought out, and loyalty tests are administered. Members testify to their own loyalty.

Authority. The group revolts overtly against the instructor, thereby transforming the fantasy of instructor-omnipotence and member-impotence into a new set of ideas concerning what members can and should do independently of the instructor. Membership entails guilt over revolt and responsibility for making decisions.

Both students and instructor now have a right and an obligation to make decisions instrumental to the group goal, and the instructor is obligated to protect those who seek to engineer such decisions. The taboo against expressing negative reactions against the instructor is attenuated.

Intimacy. The experience of learning something by collaborating results in the inhibition of intimacy is its aim; that is, being close for its own sake is differentiated from being close enough to produce something of value. The latter becomes the basis of the new normative relationship. Differences among members, as persons and in their roles, tend to become tolerable and admitted (providing there is some indication that each contributes toward effective goal reduction). Persons who remain alien in this respect become crucial issues; they either come around or are ostracized. These negotiations eventuate, first, in roles which approximate collaborating ones and, second, in an attenuation of the taboo against expressing positive feelings.

Work. Having discovered that some behavior of some members is insightful, instructive, and productive, the group attempts to follow their lead. It practices creating fantasy material and interpreting it as a means of discovering more about what is going on in the group. In another direction, it examines carefully the basic facts in cases and expresses a desire to hear tape recordings of its own procedures. On the one hand, all data (ideally) become relevant; on the other, the canons of observation, interpretation, and formulation are (ideally) retained.

EMERGENT PROPERTIES

From the viewpoint of the group as a whole, the following new components are important.

A nucleus of persons is committed to a rudimentary normative system. These norms are based both upon pragmatic tests of what the group can do and what it needs to do to accomplish its goal.

A set of conditions are formulated which members must fulfill before they take group time and before their roles are allowed to become differentiated.

A new role relationship arises between member and instructor which replaces the previous image of impotence confronting omnipotence. Members are obligated to inquire and to decide; the instructor is obliged both to protect the innovator and to back up those who exercise control in behalf of the new norms.

A new role relationship among members distinguishes the instrumental from the personal. Though obliged to work together members are not obliged to like one another nor are they prevented from doing so. Though obliged to reveal those feelings which are essential to an understanding of the cases and the groups' processes, members remain free to express or not to express those personal likes and dislikes peripheral to the group's task.

A new conception of the group's task arises. Figure and ground begin to separate. Replacing the image of a formless, boundless mass of data, projections, interpretations, and fantasies is a notion of the relevance of facts, the value of interpretations, and the fruitfulness of formulations. Usefulness replaces certainty as a criterion.

A concept arises of the group as a unique entity distinct from the constituent personalities and from all other groups. It could now be named. The boundary between group and nongroup is confirmed, as evidenced, for example, by the impossibility of admitting a stranger and by the unavoidable pain at the loss of a member.

In short, in this phase the group seeks to define and to legislate what it should be. As it evaluates, selects, and decides, it inadvertently becomes something special—it becomes a unique system with its own values, norms, internal arrangements, and outlook on the external world.

Production

ISSUES

Having become a group of a special kind, its new issue is what it can produce. Can its observations and interpretations stand up to tests against reality? Can its formulations be communicated, understood, remembered, and transmitted to others? Can it create something of lasting value?

For a member, the issues are: Can I communicate ideas which are both relevant and in such a form that they can be tested against reality? Can I hear, evaluate, and test someone else's ideas?

ACTIVITIES

Though by no means for the first time, but with new determination, members apply what they know about the processes of observation, emotional expression, interpretation, formulation, and testing.

Observation. To what extent are observations complete and accurate? What cues and signals does one tend to miss?

Emotional Expressions. To what extent are the feelings experienced by members, by authors, or by persons in the cases conveyed for what they are? What is repressed? What is distorted? What is projected?

Interpretation. On how many levels and in terms of what facets might one interpret an event? What is a statement saying about the case? about the speaker? about the group?

Formulation. By what gift or skill are ideas which come from the concrete and the particular transformed into ones which are helpful in clarifying or explaining disparate data? How does one translate what is learned into ideas that can be conveyed and tested for both their relevance and their lasting value?

Testing. By reference to basic data—whether it be tapes of their own sessions, facts as reported in cases, or of some other sort—observations, interpretations, and formulations are impersonally tested for completion, accuracy, and usefulness.

Internal Checks. Since tests show the effect of various defenses upon the working processes, the group tends to establish internal checks against denial, distortion, intellectualization, and projection. Statements are screened as they are produced, and members are ranked according to their contact with reality.

Diagnosis. Members attempt to assess what is in the here and now that either disrupts or facilitates the working process and, consequently, they seek to understand more fully how group process affects the learning process.

EMERGENT PROPERTIES

Ordinarily, the production test causes a revision of certain components:

The nature of the task is redefined. It is more difficult than it seemed.

The aspiration level of the group is lowered. The revised goal is to understand something about limited aspects of human and group processes.

Norms governing what should or should not be expressed are relaxed. ("Deviant" behavior might be productive after all.)

Central cultural themes are formed around those interpretations and formulations which have been found insightful, helpful, and apparently of lasting value. Since these themes have, in a sense, saved the group, members gather them and husband them. They symbolize what the group wishes itself to be.

The group as a whole becomes an object of negative feelings. Members are disillusioned with its resources and its potential.

At the same time, the intellectual boundaries between fact and fantasy, between group process and content of statements, between the internal group and the external objects, and between a gratifying statement and one based on reality are clearer. The distinctions have been clarified by the testing that has gone on.

In short, during this phase the group puts itself to the test of producing something of general and lasting value. Rallying around a set of central insights, salvaged from the test, it emerges disillusioned and less ambitious but intellectually keener.

Separation

Most training and learning groups run by a fixed schedule. The first and last meeting date is known. Consequently, quite irrespective of how the group has done and what it aspires to do, the fact of separation forces a complex set of demands and issues, some of which are briefly noted below.

ISSUES

Two central issues exist for the group as a whole. First, can it create something of value that will not die; and, second, how are the boundaries between the group and other objects to be dissolved in time for the last meeting?

For a member, the first issue is: How can I recollect within the allotted time my attachments to others and to the group? Second, am I able to carry away the group's valuables, as well as its finished and unfinished business?

ACTIVITIES

Work. Effort, sometimes compulsive, is spent generating new interpretations and formulations which might hold the key or the secret. The history of the group is reviewed and successful episodes are codified. Paralleling this effort is an attempt to understand what the group is (more than what it can do) by understanding the way it dies.

Intimacy. Members withdraw first by expressing their deepest feelings, positive or negative, about one another, then, by expressing positive feelings. The boundary between group members and others is dissolved by bringing friends in as visitors and by recounting fully to outside friends what is going on in the group.

Authority. The attempt to dissolve the boundary between the instructor as authority and other authorities takes the form of asking him to state once and for all that his role is artificial, not real, that the course from the beginning has been an experiment, and that if he were truly himself he would not do what he has done.

Commitment. Members review their roles and what they have given and received from one another. They seek a confirmation that their choice to join the enterprise was a wise one. Positive feelings about the experience are aroused and members thank one another for contributions.

Yearning for a benediction from some source, the group dies.

EMERGENT PROPERTIES

What is left:

A group that is dead and cannot be revived. Individual fantasies of a future reunion.

Within persons, a tendency, on occasion, to model their emotional and intellectual processes of experiencing, observing, interpreting, formulating, and so forth after the pattern of processes which occurred in the group. Individual members tend, on occasions, to operate as the group as a system operated.

A tendency in some members to create groups in which they can re-enact the instructor's role.

A tendency in some members to induce their friends to re-enact their own role by joining the course.

Angry feelings toward the instructor for beginning something he should know could not be finished. Anger toward themselves for committing themselves to such an enterprise.

Some sense of accomplishment.

LIFE CYCLE AND THE SINGLE CASE

Even with the relatively few facets caught by SPA, one can suggest, as a first approximation, the periods within the life cycle of the Harvard group. Closer approximations will require far more detailed analysis than this one affords simply because, within any period, there are both more issues than major content categories and many of the negotiations do not manifest themselves in the kind of content categorized by the scheme. Cases in point are estimates of personal commitment and of the effectiveness of work. Nonetheless, insofar as periods constitute major, distinguishable transitions from one type of system to another, one can expect traces to be detected. Although such traces show major change, they do not indicate with any precision just what is in transition.

Table 6 identifies the five life-cycle periods for the learning group under study and summarizes the changes taking place during each period in six major content-analysis indices. The *encounter*, beginning with activism and ending with retrenchment and anomie, lasts about ten sessions. As much as any other period, it is defined by content changes: The increase in neutrality is associated with a decrease in negative references. *Boundary-testing and role-modeling* proceeds, as a phase, for another 14 sessions. This expansive, confusing, exploratory period exhibits, as one might expect, fluctuations in most of the measures. Some sessions are coldly neutral and others, almost in alternation, are highly affective. On one day, the group discusses outsiders; on others, themselves; and these days alternate more frequently. Meanwhile, positive references increase. The *norm-formation* phase is introduced by the revolt against the instructor. Neutrality drops; negative increases steadily; positive increases some, then levels off; and the focus of discussion is largely *within* the

TABLE 6   INDICES OF CONTENT ACCORDING TO PERIODS IN LIFE CYCLE

Period In Life Cycle	Approximate Sessions within Period	Neutral	Negative	Positive	Locus: Internal or External	Preponderance of Negative over Positive	Relation between Internal Negative Preponderance and External Negative Preponderance
I The Encounter	1 – 10 9/30 – 10/23	Increases	Decreases	Decreases	Fluctuates	Decreases	Decrease together
II Testing Boundaries and Modeling Roles	9 – 24 10/21 – 12/2	Fluctuates	Increases, then decreases	Increases	Fluctuates	Cyclical; increase, decrease, increase	Fluctuate together
III Creating Indigenous Norms	24 – 41 11/27 – 2/26	Decreases sharply	Increases steadily	Increases to plateau	Internal	Cyclical; decrease, increase, decrease	Fluctuate together until #35; then, depart with internal negative high
IV Production	39 – 60 2/19 – 4/18	Fluctuates about a low mean, then increases	Decreases	Increases to plateau	Fluctuates radically, although mostly internal	Cyclical; decrease, increase, decrease, increase	Internal negative decreases sharply; after #48, indices are negatively correlated
V Separation	56 – 68 4/1 – 5/9	Increases, then at end decreases	Decreases moderately	Increases sharply at end	Internal increases	Decrease at end	Decrease together at end

group. From Thanksgiving, this period runs to the third week in February, including, aside from the revolt, such special events as Christmas vacation, preparation and taking of the mid-year examination (their grades give the clearest indication so far of the instructor's standards), the appearance of the two strangers, and the attack from within by a member. Having made a conditional peace with this member, the group looks into the case of Joseph, thereby beginning its phase of *work*.

For two months, interrupted only by spring vacation, the group addresses itself to its conception of its task. Neutrality is low, negative decreases, positive increases to a new plateau, and though primarily internal, locus shifts, as the occasion arises, from internal to external.

Internal affect becomes differentiated from external affect: Positive feelings are expressed internally, negative feelings externally, particularly after session 48. It is perhaps relevant that during the heart of this period members are writing their own case for submission just before spring vacation.

When the *separation* phase begins is an open question. One therapist suggested that for most groups it starts on the first day. Issues are probably intermingled in such a way that none are excluded from any period and no one pre-empts the group at any one time. However, in this instance, the gift of the personal case to the instructor certainly helps bring the process of separation into the open. The parting on the next day for vacation emphasizes it. During the subsequent period, neutrality rises some, negative declines moderately, internal orientation increases, and during the last few sessions the group becomes emphatically positive; and, as noted earlier, in contrast to the first day it refers to itself 385 times as "we," "the group," and so on. Few negative remarks are made about this dissolving collectivity.

Life-cycle models must be extended to additional levels and must be filled in with more detail. Transformations occurring within an hour's meeting must be understood and formulated; and, it would be useful to the practitioner if the notions were sufficiently precise to handle changes from moment to moment. However, no matter how refined, conceptions of system change will be only one part of general group theory. Other portions will want to emancipate themselves from transformation *of* structure and deal directly with dynamic mechanisms *within* the structure, mechanisms which operate regardless of the stage of development of the system. As an analogy, the usefulness of the notion of a life cycle in the study of human organisms does not detract from the fruitful study of principles of internal dynamics, analytically independent of the developmental stage. One may discover, for example, some differences in the circulatory system of the neonate and the aged, but it is important that certain principles hold for both. In far more rudimentary terms, the next chapter turns to two dynamic principles, or mechanisms, of group process, brings data of SPA to bear upon them, and suggests points to be included in a general theory.

6

Two Dynamic Issues

As group events in their moment-by-moment occurrence depart from randomness, principles of order of some sort are suggested. When there is reason to believe that these principles entail a number of simultaneously operating forces or variables, an interrelated system exists. Group dynamics is no more and no less than a set of statements about such principles. The first of two which concern us in this chapter is introduced by Bales in his hypothesis of the opposition between adaptive and integrative changes.[1] An examination of this hypothesis as an appropriate explanation for sign-process data leads to the observation that it is only partially applicable because signs of integrative efforts are confounded with signs of loyalties to other groups. The discussion suggests that small groups are open, not closed, systems. One theoretical implication of this suggestion is that exchanges *between* systems are as necessary to understand as exchanges *within* a system.

The second issue concerns the mechanisms which mediate group behavior, on the one hand, and thoughts, images, and feelings ex-

---

[1] Robert F. Bales, "Adaptive and Integrative Changes as Sources of Strain in Social Systems," in *Small Groups,* eds. A. Paul Hare, Edgar F. Borgatta, and Robert F. Bales (New York: Alfred A. Knopf, Inc., 1955), p. 127.

pressed by members, on the other. How are interpersonal processes related to views taken of, or feelings expressed about, external matters? Are inputs to group culture (those inputs dealing with external matters) dynamically connected with the interpersonal structure? Does a group, in creating its culture, see the outside world in its own light, such that trusting members see a trusting world and conflicting ones see external dissension? Or does a group employ displacement, such that a hostile world is associated with internal solidarity? By what mechanism, or mechanisms, are internal behavioral processes related to thoughts and images of the outside? The correlation of internal and external SPA scores leads to the tentative suggestion that this dynamic alters as groups move through the life cycle.

ADAPTIVE AND INTEGRATIVE CHANGES

Looking at large-scale social systems in a very abstract way, one can form an idea of two "chains of events" or "series of strains" starting from opposite poles and in opposite directions, tending to cancel each other out, and each in its terminal effects tending to set off the opposite chain of events. One chain of events has its starting point in the necessities of adaptation to the outer situation and proceeds in its series of strains through changes in the division of labor, changes in the distribution of property, authority, and status, and has its malintegrative terminal effects in the disturbance of the existing state of solidarity. The other chain of events has its starting point in the necessities of integration or reintegration of the social system itself and proceeds in its series of strains through a reactive (or perhaps aboriginal) emphasis on solidarity which exerts a dissolving, undermining, equalizing, or curbing effect on the differential distribution of status, on differences in authority, differences in distribution of property, and differences in functional roles in the division of labor, with an ultimate effect that may be maladaptive. The social system with its organization, we postulate, tends to swing or falter indeterminately back and forth between these two theoretical poles: optimum adaptation to the outer situation at the cost of internal malintegration or optimum internal integration at the cost of maladaptation to the outer situation.[2]

For small groups, Bales suggests that response to task-demands introduces a tendency to divide labor and to evaluate differential

---

[2] Bales, "Adaptive and Integrative Changes," in *Small Groups*, pp. 127-28.

preference differentially and that this, in turn, strains the solidary relations among members: "As particular functional problems (instrumental, adaptive, integrative, or expressive) become more acute . . . strains are created toward the definition of specific roles. . . ."[3] Valued performance leads to increased status, to an added increment of rewards, and to preferential access to resources. Progressive differentiation and inequality lead to more centralized control, resulting in a still more highly differentiated system.

> . . . As status differences between persons increase strains are created toward a less solid (more neutral, indifferent, or antagonistic) relation between them. Thus, to conclude, as the functional roles performed by persons in a group become more specific, differentiated, and formal, strains are created toward a less solidary relation between them.[4]

From the other pole, solidarity among members tends to undermine differentiation, to merge status differences, and to depress mobility.

> As solidarity between persons performing specific, differentiated, and formal roles increases, strains are created toward a more diffuse, less differentiated, and less formalized performance of functional social roles, which may in turn be accompanied by a loss of efficiency and responsibility, a loss of the inducement of increased status, a perversion of function from group ends to the individual ends of the persons immediately involved, and so may threaten the adaptation and integration of the group as a whole.[5]

In summary, as ". . . interpersonal solidarity increases . . . strains are created toward insecurity through the threat of a less effective adaptation of the system as a whole to the outer situation. . . ."[6]

Reactions are expected against movements either toward the adaptive or the solidary pole. In the first case, "One of the possible reactions . . . is a reactive, compulsive attempt to secure and retain symbols of love, acceptance, solidarity and the initiation of rituals and fantasies on this theme. . . ."[7] In the second, Bales illustrates possible reactions by reference to phenomena in larger social

---

[3] Bales, "Adaptive and Integrative Changes," in *Small Groups*, p. 128.
[4] Bales, "Adaptive and Integrative Changes," in *Small Groups*, p. 128.
[5] Bales, "Adaptive and Integrative Changes," in *Small Groups*, p. 130.
[6] Bales, "Adaptive and Integrative Changes," in *Small Groups*, p. 131.
[7] Bales, "Adaptive and Integrative Changes," in *Small Groups*, p. 129.

systems, such as limitation of contact, avoidance, and physical segregation.

In short, task effort separates members, who then seek signs of solidarity; closeness undermines the instrumental task performance, which then demands distance between members.

Does the learning group exhibit such swings from one pole to the other? Four points pertain in applying the hypothesis to the learning group.

First, it is important to note that Bales uses the concept "adaptive" in a most abstract sense. It refers to the *existence* of a problem (and response to it) rather than to the nature of the problem. In shifting from a larger system to small groups, the referent of "adaptation to the outer situation" becomes orientation to functional problems, whether the problems themselves are "adaptive," instrumental, integrative, or expressive. Presumably, as any group issue becomes pressing, acute, and in need of solution, the chain of hypothetical strains upon solidarity is "set off." The significance of this effect in applying the hypothesis to a concrete case is that, providing there are unresolved problems and providing members do not withdraw from the field, one may expect strain on solidarity quite apart from the specific nature of the problem.

Correspondingly, providing interpersonal attachments persist, the undermining effect of expressions of solidarity would be expected to occur regardless of which functional problem might be involved. The advantages of this highly abstract formulation is that its dynamic relation does not depend upon the system being at a certain stage or upon its functional problem being of a certain nature. Regardless of transformations or of functional orientation, it leads one to expect the system "to swing or falter indeterminately back and forth between these two theoretical poles." Consequently, though our examination of current data may refer to the issue before the group, the applicability of the hypothesis does not depend upon it.

Second, according to the hypothesis, a swing toward the problem-solving pole is accompanied or followed closely by manifestations of interpersonal strains, which in turn are followed by manifestations of reconfirmation of solidarity. If it is assumed that both commitment to the group (and to resolving its issues) and interpersonal attachments remain constant, then one would predict a cyclical movement in the *manifestations* of swings from one pole to the other. Manifestations are, first, of interpersonal strain, and second, of reconfirmation of solidarity.

Third, it can be argued that the measure from SPA which best estimates the existence of strain within the group is the total frequency of negative references, including both those references to group members and to outside objects. Correspondingly, the appropriate measure estimating reconfirmation of solidarity is the total frequency of positive comments. The reason for using the total frequency is that, as stated above, members often express strain in an indirect fashion. Symbolically, the conflict among persons in a case may refer to group members: As the instructor sits upon his desk, alone and apart, members express their distaste of Mrs. Michaelson, who divides the house into "mine" and "theirs." Processes within the here and now may be expressed as existing in the there and then. Likewise, affection for outsiders may well be a poetic entreaty to one's fellow member. Total measures are assumed to reflect the feelings of antagonism or solidarity regardless of the symbolic mechanism which might be employed. Consequently, an increase in stress, however indirectly manifested, will be detected by the total negative readings; and an increase in the desire to reconfirm solidarity will be detected by the total positive readings, quite apart from symbolic mechanisms.

Fourth, and finally, in respect to empirical measures, the index used to trace the adaptive-integrative movement is the balance between total negative and positive references. It was noted previously that negative references have their own course through the group's life cycle. In general, they increase, then decrease. Likewise, positive references have their own, though different, course. Generally, they increase in three steps. One way of minimizing the life-cycle effect is to deal, not with absolute frequencies, but with the preponderance of one type of reference over the other. For this reason, the total positive is subtracted from the total negative, giving a preponderance of negative for each session, and the three-session moving average is plotted. This curve is presented in Chart 6. A point above the zero horizontal represents more negative than positive; a point below, the reverse.

The first striking feature of the curve is its cyclical pattern. Falling to a trough around the 7th session, negative preponderance rises to

CHART 6   PREPONDERANCE OF NEGATIVE EXPRESSIONS
           OVER POSITIVE EXPRESSIONS

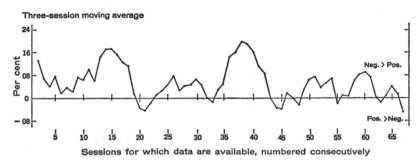

Sessions for which data are available, numbered consecutively

a peak around the 15th, falls again to the 21st, rises and declines again to the 23rd (the last session of the first term). Mounting to another peak around the 38th, it declines to the 45th. It rises again, only to drop abruptly, until it reaches its lowest point around the last session. The second feature is the regularity of peaks and troughs, especially the first four sets which are roughly equidistant. Third, if the curve for the period from session 12 to 33 is laid over the curve from session 35 to 55, it will be seen that they are almost identical. That is, if we take away the first 12 sessions and the final 12 sessions (in both of which, negative decreases), there remain 2 sets of major and minor peaks which are almost identical. Fourth, during each term the preponderance of negative decreases, more so in the second term than in the first. The group ends on its most positive note of the year. Our discussion begins with the cyclical pattern.

The fit between movements in the curve and predictions from the Balesian hypothesis seems close. Before concluding that the hypothesis accounts for the cycles, let us ask if any factors, other than problem-solving and resolidification, might account for the readings. To do this, we examine what was going on in the group just during the peaks and then during the troughs.

Again, notes on the six peaks are as follows: (1) during the first few sessions, talk is about persons outside the group, Mrs. Michaelson, and so on; the negative is external and focused upon a parental figure; (2) around the 14th or 15th session, discussion is again about external persons and again about parental figures—Mr. and Mrs.

Thomas—the negative focusing chiefly upon the husband; (3) many processes are at play around the period from the 26th to the 30th session: Christmas vacation, leader is absent, discussion of Freud's case of *Little Hans*, and so on; reference is largely internal, and negative expressions toward the instructor reach their peak; (4) at the peak on the 38th session—the attack by a member and the discussion of Joseph and his brothers occurred—reference shifts midway through this peak from internal to external; (5) at the 51st session, the substitute instructor leads a discussion of a case about the fate of a wife and family after the death of her husband; external references are relatively high; (6) at 60, the instructor is again absent, and orientation is almost wholly internal.

During the first two peaks, reference is to external authority figures; for the third, reference is internal, and negative to instructor reaches its maximum. During the fourth, reference is first internal then abruptly external, peers being involved in both. During the remaining two peaks when the instructor is away, reference in the first is external; in the second, internal.

In line with the argument in Chapter 4, the three peaks during the first term are manifestations of having engaged the authority issue—first mainly through cases, then as the term draws to an end, directly with the instructor. Again, as suggested above, the first major peak of the second term represents an engagement with the peer issue, first within the group, then in the case of Joseph and his brothers.

If these interpretations are correct, they indicate, first, that the group was directly engaged with basic group issues during the negative peaks and, second, that, as they shift the locus from external to internal and the subject from authority to intermember relations, the magnitude of the negative peaks increase. The first directly supports, and the second is not inconsistent with, the Balesian hypothesis.

Quite another picture appears, however, regarding the troughs. Although the instructor did not take attendance every day, he noted the times when it was conspicuously low and, of course, noted on the record when he himself was absent. A review shows that, except for the first, all troughs occur either when many members are absent (de facto separation) or just before the group is to disperse (anticipated separation), or when there is both de facto and anticipated separation.

The first trough, as seen above, corresponds to retrenchment—high neutrality and academic discussion of the readings. During the second trough, the instructor is absent; the group discusses *Russ May*, and attendance is low because of Thanksgiving. The dip at the 27th session occurs just before departure for Christmas vacation, and the major trough at the 33rd session is at the end of the term—attendance is low on both occasions. At the 44th, the instructor is absent with no substitute, and at the 45th, only 9 members of the class are present. Again, at the 56th—the day before spring vacation—only 9 members are present. At the 63rd and at the last session, attendance is again low—8 for the 63rd and 8 for the last day.

By and large, troughs coincide with positive peaks discussed in Chapter 3, where we noted their association with anticipated separation. To this observation can now be added the fact that attendance was frequently low for sessions just before dispersal. On these occasions, separation is de facto as well as anticipated.

As suggested earlier, one consequence of being a partial group is a feeling of loss. Certain members are totally unavailable. Members may feel that the group is disintegrating, unable to keep itself intact. In response, members may try to consolidate what remains and to express enough solidarity to keep the group alive. Before the break at mid-year, they plan a party; on the last day, a fall reunion on the banks of the Charles. Feeling torn apart, the group tries to pull itself together.

This connection between de facto or anticipated separation and positive references constitutes an alternative to the Balesian hypothesis as an explanation of the troughs. From the former viewpoint, troughs are not caused by reactions to adaptive-instrumental efforts but by an effort to counteract an immediate or anticipated loss. Positive swings are not reactions to negative swings but, instead, are responses to the fact that the group is not, or will not, be together.[8]

---

[8] Warren G. Bennis, "Defenses Against 'Depressive Anxiety' in Groups: The Case of the Absent Leader," *Merrill-Palmer Quarterly of Behavior and Development,* VII (1961), 3-30.

Absences remind members, as well as students of groups, that the group is neither complete unto itself nor detached from other systems but instead is interlaced with them. Processes in the group are subject to processes within this more complex network. Absences signal loyalties—greater loyalties—to systems other than the group (one's family, one's friends, other courses, other interests). A frequent fantasy upon the absence of the leader, for example, is that he has abandoned this group for another he likes better. Positive expressions on such occasions are, among other things, efforts to confirm the loyalty felt toward the local group.

Accordingly, the observed cyclical movement occurs because of the group's interrelationship with other segments of society. It results from alternating demands, first, from commitment to the group's task (negative peak), then from reactions to commitments to other systems (positive peaks). Regularity of peaks and troughs may be accounted for by the regularity of absences or separations, which in turn are due to the regularity of the academic calendar —or put another way, due to the regularity with which other systems demand an expression of loyalty. In short, the swings are between two poles: this group and systems other than this group. The regularity is determined by factors which ramify into an ancient chronology and an institutionalized provision that various collectivities of a society have their season.

Even so, the matter seems more complicated. Although absences and anticipated separation may account for positive readings at the pit of the trough, declines from peak to trough are gradual. In some instances, they begin two weeks before the trough—too long a period to be explained by the mechanics of three-session moving averages or, possibly, by de facto separation. What transpires from peak to trough seems, therefore, to be the compound of a number of factors. Do members unconsciously pace their instrumental efforts this far in advance of departure so that they will not take on more than they can handle? As positive begins to increase over negative, do members stay away as a means of avoiding hypersolidarity? Or, on the other hand, are absences an invulnerable means of expressing negative feelings toward the group? These questions lead to an explanation which accounts for the decline and trough either in terms of internal processes or in terms of competitive commitments to other relations, collectivities, and interests. Whether explanations refer to the internal or to the external, it is entirely possible that both are operating such that Balesian reintegrative attempts precede de facto and anticipated separation. In any case, the data indicate the inadequacy of an explanation based solely upon the immediate group as a closed system.

To summarize, the preponderance of total negative over total positive references exhibits a strikingly regular cyclical pattern. The adaptive-integrative hypothesis of Bales—which anticipates such a cycle—seems applicable as an explanation of negative peaks. However, because troughs occur either when attendance is low, the instructor is absent, or just before dispersal of the group, they may be interpreted as attempts to hold together a dispersing or dispersed group rather than as reintegrative efforts in response to instrumental efforts. Even so, this alternative hypothesis is not entirely satisfactory because declines to troughs are quite gradual and therefore are underway some time before dispersal. Whether these gradual declines are due to a Balesian reaction to previous instrumental effort or to an anticipation of future separation is not clear. However, in any case, the cyclical movement seems due to factors which compound internal forces with reactions to external commitments.

The implication for group theory is simple and important. *Small groups are not closed systems.* A theory of their dynamics must extend beyond the immediate scene and incorporate those demands which make themselves felt in a systematic way upon the immediate scene.

Counting waking and sleeping hours, members of this learning group spend, at best, less than two per cent of their week in the group. Members have many other commitments: their personal interests; friends; other classes; religious, political, familial, peer, and many other associations. Reference-group theory has helped emphasize the fact that a member may refer privately to one of these units as a basis for his beliefs and standards. As essentially part of the same process, he may express within the group strains (or satisfactions, as the case may be) which are born elsewhere—just as he may wait until he is in other contexts before he overtly manifests internal processes begun within the group. This *conveyance* on the part of members renders the group a nontotal institution. That to which and from which there is conveyance is within the *field* of the group and, as such, is part of its periphery. There is no question that ramifying the group into this often widely dispersed field complicates theory-building; but, on the other hand, bounding the group by physical walls and by what can be seen and heard must leave many processes unexplained.

This barrier is especially obvious when connections to external collectivities are not idiosyncratic but instead are common among members and reactions to them are shared, scheduled, and routinized. Christmas vacation is one of the clearest of many examples: The university closes down; all ways are opened for a return home; there is no choice of meeting or not meeting; separation is enforced; there can be no giving and getting from the group during this period; group process is suspended. The giving and getting—the gift exchange—is in another context among other authorities and peers. Traces of the group are taken to the family, and family traces are returned. There is an exchange, but the unequivocal act of moving from one collectivity to another as an acknowledgment of loyalty to the second is what makes the exchange possible. Just what loyalty is felt may be important for some investigators. The more general point, however, is that *provision* for the move, for taking traces to the family, for re-enacting facts of the group's process and returning with new traces—*society's provision* for this is patterned. Society's calendar schedules a particular impact upon the group. Without meeting, its members go through similar experiences; without meeting, the group changes in systematic ways. These patterned influences during dispersal of a group need to be brought within the field of group theory.

INTERACTION AND CONTENT

The second dynamic problem concerns the mechanisms which relate interpersonal process with the thoughts, images, desires, and fantasies produced by the interacting persons. Projective techniques in personality research are based upon the assumption that intrapsychic processes, not otherwise obvious, are represented symbolically in fantasy. Just how symbol and process are related is, of course, a matter of great importance to the psychologist. It is important to know, for example, whether success imagery refers to internal satisfaction over achieving one's goal or to a wish that one experience fewer failures. In one case, there is what might be called a positive association between imagery and process; in the other, a negative one.

Though by no means as sophisticated, conceptually or technically, efforts have been made to apply the psychologist's assumption about personality to the study of group process.[9] Might not a group's structure and dynamics be conveyed in symbolic form in the content of the group's culture? The clinical observer notes frequently that talk about others—whether they be animals, neighbors, the government, or persons in the cases—is in one sense talk about the group itself. A group slowly disintegrating becomes interested in the League of Nations; one blocking on its past history becomes preoccupied with Proust; one facing an examination imagines how it would be to have a "real blow-out of a party"; another, doubtful as to what it should do and anxious about who is who, creates an army story, the characters being given duty and rank and eventually being overtly identified with particular group members.

The general theoretical issue is how cultural content—and the processes of accumulating cultural content—is related to the social structure and to interaction processes of a group. Are symbolic representations inspired by the structure of relations? Do they in some way reflect the structure?

Though perhaps in a different guise, symbolic content in group discussion contains the seeds of the cultural forms recognizable in the larger society as religion, technology, philosophy, and so on. Thus, from this theoretical viewpoint, study of connections between structure and content on the small-group level parallels the long-standing and general sociological issue of the relationship between social system and culture.

Practically, understanding the connection between talk about "others" and group processes is important to group clinician, systematic observer, and small-group experimenter alike. The clinician needs to interpret immediately what is going on. If content and process are positively associated, that is, if preoccupation with dissension in others reflects latent dissension among members, the interpretation and possible intervention of the clinician should be one

---

[9] W. E. Henry and H. Guetzkow, "Group Projection Sketches for the Study of Small Groups," *Journal of Social Psychology*, XXXIII (1951), 77-102; and also Guetzkow and Henry, *Group Projective Sketches* (Ann Arbor: University of Michigan Press, 1949).

thing; whereas, if they are negatively associated, so that preoccupation with solidarity among outsiders expresses its lack among members, then interpretation and intervention should be another. For his part, the systematic observer needs to know this connection to understand the "meaning" his findings have for group dynamics. The matter is also important for the experimenter. If group forces, such as tension, are manifest partly in overt behavior and partly in symbolic form, or alternatively, if they are manifest inversely in each sector, he must know these connections in order to conclude accurately the existence and amount of such forces.

Compared to personality research, there is a certain advantage in dealing with the issue on the group level. More of the relevant material—but by no means all or even enough of it—is available to the observer. Members interact as they produce content. The correspondence between this part of group process and the content of its imagery regarding external objects can, therefore, be compared more easily than can private, internal processes and overt imagery.

When a group presents its own processes in the portrayal of processes about outsiders, this relationship can be called *projection.* The outside world is cast in a light corresponding to the state of the internal system, and, as in the case of individual projection, the original processes remain within the system. This is the basis for the observer's interpretation that talk about animals is talk about the group If we press the matter further, to the point where we collect data regarding what is done within the group and what is said about others, the inference of the clinical observer amounts to the proposition that processes within the group correspond to processes portrayed about others. Concretely and empirically, this means that interaction among members (whether they are aware of it or not) is positively associated with the group's depiction of interaction among outsiders. Consequently, the balance of internal negative should be positively associated with the balance of external negative.

Effective displacement is a second and distinctly different mechanism. The distressed group projects its problems (for example, its intermember hostility) upon external objects and by this means relieves itself (of interpersonal hostility), with the result that the outside world is cast in a light opposite its own internal processes. Quarrels among outsiders are rallying points for solidarity among members; affection depicted elsewhere reflects dissension in the here and now.

In this case, the internal, interpersonal processes stand in an inverse relationship to those processes attributed to external persons. Hypothetically, an increase in negative attributes outside is expected to be accompanied by positive interaction; and an increase in positive external referents, accompanied by negative interaction among members. *Effective* displacement, to repeat, eventuates in an inverse relationship between internal and external attributions.

Inasmuch as SPA separates internal and external objects, and classifies referents to each in the same positive, negative, and neutral terms, it permits a preliminary test concerning which of these mechanisms operate in the Harvard group. Preliminary, first, because there is no pretension that all the more subtle, latent group processes are represented by analysis of content, and second, because, as mentioned earlier, external referents are influenced by other factors, such as the actual material in the cases.

To test for the mechanisms, let us first separate internal from external references, then, for *each realm,* calculate the difference between negative and positive expressions. A preponderance of negative-internal represents an overbalance of negative to positive evaluations, feelings, and acts among members; that is, disagreement is higher than agreement, and aggression is higher than manifest signs of acceptance. Correspondingly, a preponderance of external references means that there are more negative than positive thoughts, images, and ideas about outsiders; that is, conflict is discussed more than conciliation, and the distasteful person is talked about more than an admired one.

A positive association between these two indices, as they change session by session, supports the hypothesis that projection is employed: The internal system and the external world are similar. A negative association supports the displacement hypothesis: The outside world is the antithesis of the internal.

The three-session moving averages of each of the two indices are presented in Chart 7. Although first term, session-by-session *shifts* are not statistically associated (only 13 of the 31 shifts are in the same direction), the curves follow one another closely. The major departures (between 9 and 15) occur as both curves are generally

CHART 7   PREPONDERANCE OF NEGATIVE OVER POSITIVE AFFECT
REGARDING THE INTERNAL SYSTEM COMPARED WITH
PREPONDERANCE OF NEGATIVE OVER POSITIVE AFFECT
REGARDING THE EXTERNAL SITUATION

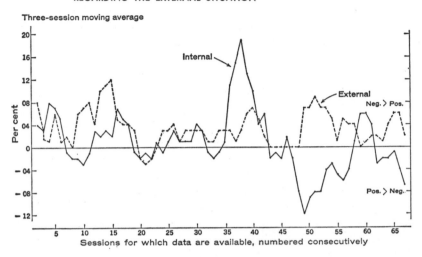

Three-session moving average

Sessions for which data are available, numbered consecutively

increasing. The second term presents a different picture. The curves
begin to depart almost immediately, and from the 48th to the 63rd
session they move generally in opposite directions. The average differences between the 2 curves taken session by session before
smoothing are: first term, .07; and second term, .10; though again
this difference is not significant.

Certainly, if effective displacement were in force during the fall
term, the internal balance would not follow the external as closely
as it does. After the 9th session, one would expect a shift toward
the positive, rather than the observed negative increase; and, again,
after the 16th session, one would expect a shift opposite from the one
observed. Though it is questionable whether the data warrant a
firm conclusion that *projection is occurring*, it can be concluded that
effective displacement is not. Similarly, for the spring, although
there are not enough instances of displacement (of opposite shifts
in the internal and external areas) to conclude that it is the principal mechanism, it is clear that projection alone is not operating.
Moreover, between the 48th and 63rd sessions, the curves are
roughly opposite; thus, displacement seems to operate during that

limited period. This fact, plus the fact that the difference between the two curves (though not always their slopes) is somewhat greater in the second than in the first term, suggests that the dynamics can also be different.

Apparently for this group, and perhaps more generally, the question is not simply whether a positive or a negative association exists between interaction and content, but a question of the conditions under which each occurs. Subject to their limitations, the data indicate that *projection* occurs earlier in the life of the group than does *displacement*. There are reasons why this order may hold for most newly formed groups.

Displacement, a more complex mechanism than projection, requires a more sophisticated system for its operation. Effective displacement means that the direction of negative feelings toward an external object is accompanied by the release and expression of positive feelings within the group. This displacement requires, first of all, a lack of inhibition in expressing such feelings. It was suggested previously that a taboo against their expression exists in this and in similar groups, and that in time it becomes partially relieved. Until it is lifted, one would expect external negative to be accompanied by *inhibited* internal positive; whereas afterwards, one would expect it to be accompanied by overtly expressed internal positive. Consequently, if our earlier argument is valid, one of the conditions enabling displacement does not exist originally and must, therefore, develop. The same is true for the expression of internal negative feelings. In the latter case, effective displacement means that external positive expressions are accompanied by internal negative ones. Although these latter feelings may exist, they are not apt to be overtly expressed unless there is an assurance that members doing so will not jeopardize themselves. Only after considerable boundary-testing does this sense of protection develop. Consequently, only after some time can there prevail the second condition enabling displacement. A third necessary condition for the mechanism is the existence of a boundary differentiating the internal from the external. "Others" cannot be used in displacement until one differentiates between the self and others. A group cannot consolidate because of an external attack until a boundary between itself and other systems is clearly defined. It was suggested on page 72 that the boundaries regarding member, instructor, and other systems are accomplishments, rather than given facts. In many respects, the group creates itself by finding and defining itself; only after it has been defined can it know what actually constitutes the boundary between itself and things external. For the group under consideration, three important historical events are critical in this process: (1) the revolt early in December, (2) confrontation with the strangers at the beginning of the second term, and (3) the attack from the inside, following shortly thereafter. After making peace with the instructor, with themselves regarding hostile outsiders, and with themselves regarding their most hostile fellow member, the group has a clearer awareness of its identity. As it learns more nearly what it is and what it isn't, the group can begin to employ internal-external mechanisms. Until then, attempts will be dissipated by lack of distinctions.

Before conflictful issues regarding authority, peer relations, orientation to the task, and relations with other systems have been worked through, discussion of external matters, such as cases and readings, simply amounts to a substitute context (and Slater suggests a safer one) for exploring, testing out, seeking limits, and preparing for negotiation on these unresolved internal issues. Mrs. Michaelson and Mr. Thomas are not objects of effectively displaced feelings but are substitute characters in a play designed to find out what the instructor is like. Internal matters are *explored* in an external setting instead of being effectively displaced there. Though the motivation may be to resolve organizational, normative, and emotional issues, the "bleeding" from internal to external occurs because boundaries have not yet been established. Later, as the group becomes distinct, the culture of the group does not confuse Mr. Thomas with the instructor, Jane in the case with Mary Jane in the class, and Joseph of the Bible with Joe at the center of the table, although private associations may, of course, continue. Group discussion separates, for example, the "projected" elements in comments on Joseph from the more "real" elements—separates, in other words, the group from the case. Having effectively separated these two classes of elements, it may now show admiration for the ancient Joseph without suggesting that it is Joe at the center of the table who is indirectly being admired. In fact, in recognizing the difference between Joseph and Joe, it may express its dissatisfaction with the latter.

In summary, projection at the group level is a more primitive mechanism than is effective displacement. Although projection may occur before the group has distinguished among its parts and between itself and other social objects, effective displacement cannot. Displacement is possible only when boundaries exist and both anger and affection can be expressed.

These points suggest an interdependence between such mechanisms and periods in the life cycle. The weight of the still inconclusive evidence for the learning group suggests that projection is employed for a very long period—during which boundaries are slowly being established—that, later, as the group enters the productive state, displacement is employed; and that, finally, as the group prepares to disband and begins to dissolve its boundaries, projection is again employed. If the various bases of this interpretation are correct, its implication for general group theory is that, although the mechanisms refer to dynamics *in* the group, they depend upon the existence of certain conditions *of* the group. These conditions may appear or disappear as the group transforms. It becomes important to spell out the necessary and sufficient conditions for the operation of these dynamics and to compare the conditions with those prevailing during each stage of the life cycle. As progress is made on this problem, it should be possible to suggest a set of probabilities for employing certain dynamic principles as the group moves through the life cycle.

7

Summary and Conclusions

This final chapter summarizes what was done and what was learned from the study, draws three implications for group-process theory, and suggests two steps to help bridge the gap between clinician and systematic observer of groups.

THE GROUP

The study is of a single group which meets three times a week, for sixty-eight scheduled sessions, over an eight-month period. Composed of sixteen men and women students from Harvard and Radcliffe Colleges, the group is one of four sections of an academic course, the purpose of which is to develop skills in observing and interpreting concrete instances of human behavior. Subject matter consists of written cases and of the group's own processes. Active responsibility for exploring the material rests upon the students, the instructor's interventions being designed to overcome blocks to this work, to encourage exploration on a number of different levels (latent as well as manifest, symbolic as well as explicit), and to engender a setting in which members feel safe in the face of the uncertainties of their task and their own process. Students take an hour examination on outside reading materials in the fall and a mid-year and final examination on the readings, cases, and the group's proceedings. In the spring they each write a case from their own personal experience which they present, with an analysis, as a term paper.

CONTENT ANALYSIS

The proceedings are tape-recorded and all statements are classified by a method called Sign Process Analysis (SPA). The scheme abstracts the following characteristics of each statement: (1) the nature of objects referred to: *internal* or *external, male* or *female, superior* or *subordinate;* and (2) the type of cultural standard employed: *positive* if the standard is of the good, the desirable, the pleasing, the loving, the constructive; *negative* if the standard is of the evil, the undesirable, the unpreferred, the distasteful, the hating, the destructive; and *neutral* if the standard is independent of preferences and values.

Since statements often connect several objects, a further distinction is made between principal and secondary objects, a distinction which most often parallels the grammatical one of subject and object in sentences. A standard object matrix is constructed with principal objects classified along rows and secondary objects along columns, each matrix cell representing a connection between types of objects; for example, between a group member (internal, male, subordinate) and Mrs. Michaelson (external, female, superior). A special column accommodates statements which refer only to one type of object ("You are right").

Furthermore, each cell is subdivided into positive, negative, and neutral classes to accommodate the type of standard associated with the statement. Thus, "I don't like Mrs. Michaelson's way of handling it," is scored under the negative class in the cell mentioned above.

In most general terms, SPA records the distribution of positive, negative, and neutral references associated with the universe of objects, objects being separated into subsets according to the simple distinctions of locus, sex, and status.

More specifically, a summary for a given session shows (1)

frequencies of positive, negative, and neutral expressions exchanged among members about one another and about the group as a whole; (2) frequencies of positive, negative, and neutral qualities of, and connections between, external objects—persons in cases, for example, or authors, one's family, other courses, physical objects, and so on; and (3) frequencies of positive, negative, and neutral linkages between internal and external objects, both linkages which represent action of the group upon outside objects and those which represent action in the other direction. Moreover, a finer breakdown according to sex and status provides frequencies of associations with types of objects within these loci.

Any number of indices may be formed from the scores, depending upon the purpose of the study. The following ones are used in the present study:

1. Percentage of negative scores, irrespective of the nature of objects referred to.

2. A similar percentage of positive scores.

3. A similar percentage of neutral scores.

4. Percentage of internal references, irrespective of standards employed.

5. A similar percentage for external references.

6. Percentage of references to subordinates regardless of standards (not charted).

7. A similar percentage for superiors (not charted).

8. The ratio of negative references (regardless of objects) to positive references (regardless of objects).

9. The ratio of internal negative references to internal positive references.

10. The ratio of external negative references to external positive references.

ISSUES AND TRENDS

Although readings of SPA scores constitute the basic data of the study, it is by no means certain just what the readings tell us about the group. As an approximation to the solution of this problem, their meaning is interpreted in terms of issues which have been singled out from experience and from formulations of clinical observers as central to groups of this order. The issues are stated, and how the group's response to the issue is likely to be manifest in SPA scores is suggested. Trends in scores are then examined.

The first issue is whether or not the group is to enter into the special role of student of human relations. Are members to remain aloof, detached, objective, intellectual, and neutral or are they to involve themselves with the emotional and evaluative processes in whatever interpersonal situation they approach? One may want to withdraw, as though the matter were too hot to handle; or, one may want to go further and deeper—on into the unconscious level of interpersonal processes. In one direction, there is neutrality; in the other, positive and negative values, norms, and feelings. The over-all trend in the percentage of neutral references is interpreted in the light of this issue. Initially the curve increases; then, for a period oscillates. After the December 2 meeting, it declines sharply and remains low until near the end of the year.

A growing awareness of the emotional and intellectual demands of the task produces the initial increase; conflict between with-drawing from it or engaging it is manifest in the oscillation; and eventual engagement with the task results in the later decrease and the sustained low level of the curve.

The second issue is whether the group can observe and analyze itself as well as outside cases. Can it introspect and from that intro-spection understand the local sources of inferences made in the course of the discussion? Trends in internal and external references are interpreted according to this question. Roughly a 50-50 balance between internal and external references is maintained until around the 20th session. Internal references thereafter increase and remain generally high, exceptions being sessions devoted chiefly to external cases. Overcoming resistance to considering the here and now ac-counts for the major shift around the 20th session.

The third issue concerns interpersonal sources of group strain: negotiating with the instructor as the authority and confronting one's peers. The fourth concerns the inherent difficulty of the task. With due regard for the fact that not all negative references are in themselves manifestations of group strain, it is suggested that the over-all trend in total negative scores indicates the existence, the generation, and the eventual alleviation of these strains. The observed increase to the 37th session results from three factors: (1) an actual increase in strain, (2) a decrease in inhibition, and (3) a growing feeling of protection in expressing negative feelings and observations. The subsequent decrease results from partial resolution of strain (and, as mentioned below, anticipation of the end of the course).

Affection is the next issue. The uninhibited expression of love for another person in the group is taboo. Only after the group has formed as a collectivity and members conceive of themselves as members of that collectivity can affection be expressed safely and legitimately. As internal and external boundaries form and as work roles become clear, affection can be acknowledged and expressed without implicating the total person. The development of these boundaries and attenuation of the taboo against positive feelings account for the observed three-step increase in positive internal references.

Termination of the group and preparation for it is the final issue. From the beginning, the group knows when it is to end; although we do not know when separation anxiety sets in, examination of the session-by-session frequencies shows that on occasions prior to vacations and examination periods, and when attendance is low or the instructor is absent, positive references tend to increase. The final increase in positive at the end of the year is interpreted as a reaction to separation. It is possible that the general decline in negative and increase in neutral are manifestations of members detaching themselves from the task and from fellow group members.

CONCEPT OF LIFE CYCLE

A comparison of these trends with current formulations of group development suggests that conceptions of such changes might be strengthened with emphasis upon the following points:

Few groups continue to develop indefinitely; instead they form and later dissolve. Therefore, more appropriate than either the notion of an ever-progressing system or the model of recurring cycles around a point of equilibrium (even though moving) is the familiar conception of the life cycle. There is change, there is movement, there may be cycles, but the inescapable reality for members and students of groups is that the group ends. Theories of group development need to expand into theories of transformation and dissolution.

Groups create an indigenous culture, including a normative system. They give up preconceived normative notions, experience normlessness, experiment with new ideas, and attempt to establish an appropriate arrangement. New, implicit contracts are negotiated; for example, between member and instructor, between members, and between the group and its surroundings. They often transform conflict, anxiety, uncertainty, and fear into workable arrangements. Because of this and other functions, norm formation and dissolution should be theoretically integrated with other processes in the life cycle.

Current formulations are based upon the principle of perfection. The group goal is achieved, whether it is therapy, training in human relations, or learning about people. Though the data from the learning group bear only indirectly on this question, they in no way suggest goal attainment. Instead they suggest the *principle of partial consummation*. The group does not learn all about people, rather it begins to learn something about learning about people. Much the same probably happens in therapy, training, and other groups as well. If so, our conceptions of the life career of groups need revision.

In Chapter 5 these points are incorporated into a sketch of the life cycle of learning groups which consists of five periods: (1) the encounter, (2) testing boundaries and modeling roles, (3) negotiating an indigenous normative system, (4) production, and (5) separation.

GROUP THEORY

What implications has this study of a single group for our thinking about groups in general? We select three points, which to some readers may simply serve as reminders of facts already known, but which, at the same time, deserve a more substantial place in our theoretical formulation of group process.

Groups Are Open, Not Closed Systems

They are open, first, because members usually belong to a number of groups in addition to the one in question. They commit part of themselves, not all of themselves, to any one group. Feelings, thoughts, and performance, in general, are influenced by external loyalties, philosophies, and habits. Conveyed through persons, these influences become part of the set of causes which determine what is and is not done in the group. Influences operate in both directions, and the group affects a member's role in other groups. In Social Relations 120, conveyance of these influences is demonstrated by the effects of Christmas vacation: The gathering of the family had new significance for students; dispersal altered the group upon its return.

Groups are open, second, because most of them are part of a larger social complex whose structure, customs, and procedures surround the group, as the university does the class; the organization, the committee; the community, the family. Practical arrangements in these larger complexes may have subtle and profound effects upon the subsystems. In Chapter 6, it was reported that Social Relations 120 exhibited a quite regular cyclical pattern in the preponderance of negative over positive references. Bales' adaptive-integration hypothesis, which implicitly assumes a closed system, does not fully explain the phenomenon. Periods of low negative and high positive, which at first may appear as attempts to consolidate the group following instrumental effort, actually occur just before vacations or when attendance is low and are, therefore, interpreted as efforts to hold together a group experiencing temporary dissolution. The *patterning* of dispersal to those other groups, which creates the observed periodicity, is determined by the calendar. In the present case, the calendar is a simple but important example of the general influence of arrangements in the larger social complex to which group events are open.

Our analysis suggests that *the network of causation extends beyond the immediate boundaries of the group.* This means that groups themselves continuously confront the functional problem of maintaining an identity and an integrity in the face of competing loyalties, influences, and cross-pressures. It means that the investigator must be prepared to trace the causes and consequences of events throughout a field of forces whose boundaries do not, and need not, coincide with boundaries as defined by group members or by the larger social complex. It means that the group theorist must deal with a variety of boundaries, some subjective and definitional, others determined by cause and effect.

It is relevant to the development of such a theory that Parsons and Smelser, though dealing with a different sort of subsystem, have, in their study of the economy and society, addressed themselves to this problem of interchange across boundaries.[1] The theoretical task remains to experiment with their formulations in the context of the small group operating, not as abstractly functional to the larger society (as the economy is adaptive for total society), but as a small collectivity connected by behavior, feelings, and ideas with persons and with other groups.

All Small Groups Die

Some die on schedule and as abruptly as the Harvard learning group, some die more gradually, and others go in bits and pieces. Group, of course, means more than a culture, more than norms, more than certain rituals, traditions, and bylaws. It means a full-bodied operating system, composed of persons who may share culture, norms, and ways of doing things, but who, at the same time, feel about one another in certain ways and interact with one another in ways that have immediate emotional and instrumental consequences. A family comes into being, proceeds through stages, and ends. It may have a name, property, progeny, symbols of itself, but, in fact, *it* as a social unit perishes—symbols of the parents, memories of progeny, abstractions of the sociologist to the contrary notwithstanding. The fact is a general one. Regimes come to an end; the king must die; and the lover knows when he is one no longer and when that relationship is dead.

The process of the dissolution of social systems presents a theoretical problem. As stated above, neither the notion of an ever-perfecting system, nor the notion of a system in equilibrium, even around a moving point, easily accommodates dissolution. New thought must be given to the question. By what processes do decommitment and decathexis occur? By what processes are internal boundaries dissolved? In what way are external boundaries diminished and eventually eliminated? The clinical cliché that "separation is always a messy business" suggests that much needs to be accomplished but rarely is. Are there both mortal and immortal parts to

---

[1] Talcott Parsons and Neil J. Smelser, *Economy and Society* (New York: The Free Press of Glencoe, Inc., 1956), especially pp. 39-100.

a group? With impending death, what new processes are generated? what new images? what new feelings about a fellow member? about the leader? Is there an attempt to transform the mortal into the immortal? How is this process related to dissolution of boundaries? It has been suggested that, "At the end, groups go back to the beginning." If so, little is understood how or why the return occurs.

Our analysis emphasizes *the need for a theory that recognizes the reality of group death.* Beyond that, it suggests that the potential for dissolution is experienced by members throughout the life cycle of the group. We observe periodic reaction to it prior to vacations, and closer examination would probably show that it is manifest in every meeting as generally and literally as in farewells: "See you again," "Au revoir," "Till we meet," and so on. If the threat of dissolution is continuous, then the theoretical need is for more than a concept of change. It is for a more basic concept, a concept of the ever present potential for the nonexistence of the system, a concept perhaps analogous to the notion of entropy in physics.

Group Mechanisms Are Contingent upon Boundaries

Are representations of the external world dynamically related to the way members interact with one another? Borrowing from personality psychology, it is suggested that when internal interaction corresponds in quality to images of the external world this relation is to be called projection, and when they are the reverse it is to be called displacement. Empirically, projection exists when a change in the preponderance of negative over positive expressions which refer internally to the group (its members, what they say and do, and so on) is paralleled by a similar change in the preponderance of negative over positive expressions which refer externally to persons in the cases and to all other outside objects. Displacement—effective displacement—exists when these changes are opposite.

Although inconclusive, the weight of the evidence suggests that projection occurs up to and until the production stage, that displacement occurs during that stage alone, and that, as the group enters the separation stage, projection again occurs. This transition and return to a former mechanism suggests that the dynamic connection between internal interaction and portrayal of the external world depends upon the stage of the group in the life cycle, which in turn depends in part upon the existence and nature of internal-external boundaries. Only after certain boundaries are formed can the more advanced mechanism of displacement be effectively employed. As boundaries become dissolved, the mechanism loses its function. Our analysis suggests that *the dynamic relationship between social-system processes and cultural content is not only contingent but specifically contingent upon the nature of system boundaries.* Furthermore, it suggests that *these boundaries form and transform in the course of the life cycle of the group.*

THE CLINICIAN
AND THE SYSTEMATIC OBSERVER

It was suggested in the Introduction that the gap separating clinician and systematician is a real one, not only in the sense that often they do not understand fully what one another is saying or doing, but that their actual or anticipated professional roles, and hence their relation to groups, are different. One is a leader, a trainer, and a teacher; the other is an observer, a classifier, and a tester of hypotheses. One is in the group; the other is symbolically partitioned from it by an invisible or an actual screen. One is obliged to intervene; the other must not. One is responsible for the group's success; the other is responsible to science. It is not surprising that intellectual differences are associated with these divergent roles.

Nonetheless, the two specialists are joined together, at least abstractly, by the relative state of our ignorance about what is going on in the groups before each of them. Since our knowledge about group process is at most embryonic, their noncomprehension provides common ground. Very likely, they also share a deeper desire to understand groups better than they do. If true, this means that each has an investment in what the other knows and can learn and teach. Beyond this order of exchange, it means that each has a vested interest in the development of a workable theory—or set of theories—about group process.

In his essay on "Procedure in a Science" (which for a number of years has been on the reading list of Social Relations 120) Henderson presents, as two of three requirements in making a science, (1) intimate, habitual, intuitive familiarity with raw processes, and

(2) a systematic means of collecting reliable and relevant facts.[2] Curiously, persons interested in groups have tended to differentiate their professional careers mainly according to these two requirements. The clinical observer and practitioner has immersed himself in group process: He "seeks a feel for it"; and the detached systematician collects his objective data.

The first step in closing the gap is an exchange of methods between specialists. On a superficial level, this may entail "communicating with one another"; on a more substantial level, however, the systematician may leave aside his manual and his scoring schemes and enter groups either as a leader or as a member but essentially as a participant observer. Correspondingly, the clinical observer may become trained in and apply a disciplined method of collecting data.

Still, adding each specialist's role to that of the other is but a first step. Closing the gap in a truer sense involves Henderson's third requirement, namely, an effective way of thinking about the phenomena. The gap itself is engaged when those who possess an intuitive familiarity and a means of gathering objective data attempt to formulate effective thought.

Just as it is not enough to exchange roles, it is probably not enough to depend upon general theorists to do the job. For one thing, they may not choose to entertain these particular problems, and for another, general formulations usually require careful translation in applying them to a particular ecology which is often not known by the general theorist. This particular alternative evades Henderson's point that the three ingredients, the three capabilities, need to be contained within one mind and one career. It is highly desirable that those building an *effective way of thinking* enjoy an *intuitive familiarity with* and possess *knowledge of objective data*.

Therefore, the second step in closing the gap requires that both clinician and systematician add to their present roles a new one: that of formulating and communicating to others the principles they believe will lead to a general theory of group process. To the role of therapist, trainer, instructor, and leader should be added the role of formulator of the nature of the system which makes therapy,

---

[2] Lawrence J. Henderson, "Procedure in a Science," *Human Relations*, I (1953), 24-39.

training, instruction, and group goal-achievement possible—a role to which students in the Harvard group often aspire. Fundamentally, the gap will be closed only when both parties are engaged in what is essentially the same enterprise: supplying Henderson's third element of effective thought.

Index

114